APPLETONS' NEW HANDY-VOLUME SERIES.

THE

ESSAYS OF ELIA.

BY

CHARLES LAMB.

FIRST SERIES.

NEW YORK:

D. APPLETON AND COMPANY,

549 AND 551 BROADWAY.

1879.

CONTENTS.

4 CONTENTS.

THE ESSAYS OF ELIA.

THE SOUTH-SEA HOUSE.

READER, in thy passage from the Bank—where thou hast been receiving thy half-yearly dividends (supposing thou art a lean annuitant like myself)—to the Flower Pot, to secure a place for Dalston, or Shacklewell, or some other suburban retreat northerly, didst thou never observe a melancholy-looking, handsome, brick-and-stone edifice, to the left—where Threadneedle Street abuts upon Bishopsgate? I dare say thou hast often admired its magnificent portals ever gaping wide and disclosing to view a grave court, with cloisters, and pillars, with few or no traces of goers-in or comers-out—a desolation something like Balclutha's.[1]

This was once a house of trade—a centre of busy interests. The throng of merchants was here—the quick pulse of gain—and here some forms of business are still kept up, though the soul be long since fled. Here are still to be seen stately porticoes; imposing staircases, offices roomy as the state apartments in palaces—deserted, or thinly peopled with a few straggling clerks; the still more sacred interiors of court and committee-rooms,

[1] I passed by the walls of Balclutha, and they were desolate.—OSSIAN.

with venerable faces of beadles, door-keepers—directors seated in form on solemn days (to proclaim a dead
dividend), at long, worm-eaten tables, that have been
mahogany, with tarnished gilt-leather coverings, sup-
porting massy silver inkstands long since dry; the oaken
wainscots hung with pictures of deceased governors and
sub-governors, of Queen Anne, and the two first mon-
archs of the Brunswick dynasty; huge charts, which
subsequent discoveries have antiquated; dusty maps of
Mexico, dim as dreams, and soundings of the Bay of
Panama! The long passages hung with buckets, appended, in idle row, to walls, whose substance might defy
any, short of the last, conflagration: with vast ranges of
cellarage under all, where dollars and pieces-of-eight
once lay, an "unsunned heap," for Mammon to have
solaced his solitary heart withal, long since dissipated,
or scattered into air at the blast of the breaking of that
famous BUBBLE.—

Such is the SOUTH-SEA HOUSE. At least, such it was
forty years ago, when I knew it, a magnificent relic!
What alterations may have been made in it since, I have
had no opportunities of verifying. Time, I take for granted, has not freshened it. No wind has resuscitated the
face of the sleeping waters. A thicker crust by this
time stagnates upon it. The moths, that were then battening upon its obsolete ledgers and day-books, have
rested from their depredations, but other light generations have succeeded, making fine fretwork among their
single and double entries. Layers of dust have accumu-
lated (a superfetation of dirt!) upon the old layers, that
seldom used to be disturbed, save by some curious finger,
now and then, inquisitive to explore the mode of book-
keeping in Queen Anne's reign; or, with less hallowed

curiosity, seeking to unveil some of the mysteries of that
tremendous HOAX, whose extent the petty peculators of
our day look back upon with the same expression of
incredulous admiration, and hopeless ambition of rivalry,
as would become the puny face of modern conspiracy
contemplating the Titan size of Vaux's superhuman plot.

Peace to the manes of the BUBBLE! Silence and des-
titution are upon thy walls, proud house, for a memo-
rial!

Situated as thou art, in the very heart of stirring and
living commerce, amid the fret and fever of speculation
—with the Bank, and the 'Change, and the India-house
about thee, in the heyday of present prosperity, with
their important faces, as it were, insulting thee, their *poor
neighbor out of business*—to the idle and merely contem-
plative, to such as me, old house! there is a charm in
thy quiet: a cessation—a coolness from business—an indolence almost cloistral—which is delightful! With
what reverence have I paced thy great bare rooms and
courts at eventide! They spoke of the past: the shade
of some dead accountant, with visionary pen in ear,
would flit by me, stiff as in life. Living accounts and ac-
countants puzzle me. I have no skill in figuring. But thy
great dead tomes, which scarce three degenerate clerks of
the present day could lift from their enshrining shelves—
with their old fantastic flourishes and decorative rubric
interlacings, their sums in triple columniations, set
down with formal superfluity of ciphers, with pious
sentences at the beginning, without which our religious
ancestors never ventured to open a book of business or
bill of lading; the costly vellum covers of some of them
almost persuading us that we are got into some better
library—are very agreeable and edifying spectacles. I

can look upon these defunct dragons with complacency. Thy heavy, odd-shaped, ivory-handled penknives (our ancestors had everything on a larger scale than we have hearts for) are as good as anything from Herculaneum. The pounce-boxes of our days have gone retrograde.

The very clerks which I remember in the South-Sea House—I speak of forty years back—had an air very different from those in the public offices that I have had to do with since. They partook of the genius of the place!

They were mostly (for the establishment did not admit of superfluous salaries) bachelors. Generally (for they had not much to do) persons of a curious and speculative turn of mind. Old-fashioned, for a reason mentioned before. Humorists, for they were of all descriptions; and, not having been brought together in early life (which has a tendency to assimilate the members of corporate bodies to each other), but, for the most part, placed in this house in ripe or middle age, they necessarily carried into it their separate habits and oddities, unqualified, if I may so speak, as into a common stock. Hence they formed a sort of Noah's ark. Odd fishes. A lay monastery. Domestic retainers in a great house, kept more for show than use. Yet pleasant fellows, full of chat—and not a few among them had arrived at considerable proficiency on the German flute.

The cashier at that time was one Evans, a Cambro-Briton. He had something of the choleric complexion of his countrymen stamped on his visage, but was a worthy, sensible man at bottom. He wore his hair, to the last, powdered and frizzed out, in the fashion which I remember to have seen in caricatures of what were termed, in my young days, *Macaronis*. He was the last of that race of beaux. Melancholy as a gibcat over his counter all the forenoon, I think I see him, making up his cash (as they call it) with tremulous fingers, as if he feared every one about him was a defaulter; in his hypochondry ready to imagine himself one; haunted, at least, with the idea of the possibility of his becoming one; his tristful visage clearing up a little over his roast neck of veal at Anderton's at two (where his picture still hangs, taken a little before his death by desire of the master of the coffee-house, which he had frequented for the last five-and-twenty years), but not attaining the meridian of its animation till evening brought on the hour of tea and visiting. The simultaneous sound of his well-known rap at the door with the stroke of the clock announcing six, was a topic of never-failing mirth in the families which this dear old bachelor gladdened with his presence. Then was his *forte*, his glorified hour! How would he chirp, and expand, over a muffin! How would he dilate into secret history! His countryman, Pennant himself, in particular, could not be more eloquent than he in relation to old and new London—the site of old theatres, churches, streets gone to decay—where Rosamond's Pond stood—the Mulberry Gardens—and the Conduit in Cheap—with many a pleasant anecdote, derived from paternal tradition, of those grotesque figures which Hogarth has immortalized in his picture of *Noon*—the worthy descendants of those heroic confessors, who, flying to this country, from the wrath of Louis XIV. and his dragoons, kept alive the flame of pure religion in the sheltering obscurities of Hog Lane, and the vicinity of the Seven Dials!

Deputy, under Evans, was Thomas Tame. He had the air and stoop of a nobleman. You would have

taken him for one, had you met him in one of the passages leading to Westminster Hall. By stoop, I mean that
gentle bending of the body forward, which, in great
men, must be supposed to be the effect of an habitual
condescending attention to the applications of their inferiors. While he held you in converse, you felt strained
to the height in the colloquy. The conference over, you
were at leisure to smile at the comparative insignificance
of the pretensions which had just awed you. His intellect was of the shallowest order. It did not reach to a
saw or a proverb. His mind was in its original state of
white paper. A sucking babe might have posed him.
What was it, then? Was he rich? Alas! no. Thomas
Tame was very poor. Both he and his wife looked outwardly gentlefolks, when I fear all was not well at all
times within. She had a neat, meagre person, which it
was evident she had not sinned in over-pampering; but
in its veins was noble blood. She traced her descent, by
some labyrinth of relationship, which I never thoroughly
understood—much less can explain with any heraldic
certainty at this time of day—to the illustrious but unfortunate house of Derwentwater. This was the secret
of Thomas's stoop. This was the thought—the sentiment—the bright, solitary star of your lives—ye mild and
happy pair—which cheered you in the night of intellect,
and in the obscurity of your station! This was to you
instead of riches, instead of rank, instead of glittering
attainments: and it was worth them all together. You
insulted none with it; but, while you wore it as a piece
of defensive armor only, no insult likewise could reach
you through it. *Decus et solamen.*

Of quite another stamp was the then accountant, John
Tipp. He neither pretended to high blood, nor, in good

truth, cared one fig about the matter. He "thought an accountant the greatest character in the world, and himself the greatest accountant in it." Yet John was not without his hobby. The fiddle relieved his vacant hours. He sang, certainly, with other notes than to the Orphean lyre. He did, indeed, scream and scrape most abominably. His fine suite of official rooms in Threadneedle Street, which, without anything very substantial appended to them, were enough to enlarge a man's notions of himself that lived in them (I know not who is the occupier of them now), resounded fortnightly to the notes of a concert of "sweet breasts," as our ancestors would have called them, culled from club-rooms and orchestras—chorus-singers—first and second violoncellos—double basses—and clarionets—who ate his cold mutton, and drank his punch, and praised his ear. He sate like Lord Midas among them. But at the desk Tipp was quite another sort of creature. Thence all ideas, that were purely ornamental, were banished. You could not speak of anything romantic without rebuke. Politics were excluded. A newspaper was thought too refined and abstracted. The whole duty of man consisted in writing off dividend warrants. The striking of the annual balance in the company's books (which, perhaps, differed from the balance of last year in the sum of £25 1s. 6d.) occupied his days and nights for a month previous. Not that Tipp was blind to the deadness of *things* (as they call them in the city) in his beloved house, or did not sigh for a return of the old stirring days when South-Sea hopes were young—(he was indeed equal to the wielding of any the most intricate accounts of the most flourishing company in these or those days)—but to a genuine accountant the difference of proceeds is as nothing. The fractional farthing is as dear to his heart as the thousands which stand before it. He is the true actor, who, whether his part be a prince or a peasant, must act it with like intensity. With Tipp form was everything. His life was formal. His actions seemed ruled with a ruler. His pen was not less erring than his heart. He made the best executor in the world; he was plagued with incessant executorships accordingly, which excited his spleen and soothed his vanity in equal ratios. He would swear (for Tipp swore) at the little orphans, whose rights he would guard with a tenacity like the grasp of the dying hand, that commended their interests to his protection. With all this there was about him a sort of timidity—(his few enemies used to give it a worse name)—a something which, in reference to the dead, we will place, if you please, a little on this side of the heroic. Nature certainly had been pleased to endow John Tipp with a sufficient measure of the principle of self-preservation. There is a cowardice which we do not despise, because it has nothing base or treacherous in its elements; it betrays itself, not you: it is mere temperament; the absence of the romantic and the enterprising; it sees a lion in the way, and will not, with Fortinbras, "greatly find quarrel in a straw," when some supposed honor is at stake. Tipp never mounted the box of a stage-coach in his life; or leaned against the rails of a balcony; or walked upon the ridge of a parapet; or looked down a precipice; or let off a gun; or went upon a water-party; or would willingly let you go, if he could have helped it; neither was it recorded of him that, for lucre, or for intimidation, he ever forsook friend or principle.

Whom next shall we summon from the dusty dead, in

whom common qualities become uncommon? Can I forget thee, Henry Man, the wit, the polished man of letters, the *author*, of the South-Sea House? who never enteredst thy office in a morning, or quittedst it in mid-day—(what didst *thou* in an office?)—without some quirk that left a sting! Thy gibes and thy jokes are now extinct, or survive but in two forgotten volumes, which I had the good fortune to rescue from a stall in Barbican, not three days ago, and found thee terse, fresh, epigrammatic, as alive. Thy wit is a little gone by in these fastidious days—thy topics are staled by the "new-born gauds" of the time; but great thou usedst to be in Public Ledgers, and in Chronicles, upon Chatham, and Shelburne, and Rockingham, and Howe, and Burgoyne, and Clinton, and the war which ended in the tearing from Great Britain her rebellious colonies—and Keppel, and Wilkes, and Sawbridge, and Bull, and Dunning, and Pratt, and Richmond—and such small politics.—

A little less facetious, and a great deal more obstreperous, was fine, rattling, rattle-headed Plumer. He was descended—not in a right line, reader (for his lineal pretensions, like his personal, favored a little of the sinister bend)—from the Plumers of Hertfordshire. So tradition gave him out; and certain family features not a little sanctioned the opinion. Certainly old Walter Plumer (his reputed author) had been a rake in his days, and visited much in Italy, and had seen the world. He was uncle, bachelor-uncle, to the fine old Whig still living, who has represented the county in so many successive Parliaments, and has a fine old mansion near Ware. Walter flourished in George the Second's days, and was the same who was summoned before the House of Commons about a business of franks, with the old Duchess of Marlborough. You may read of it in Johnson's "Life of Cave." Cave came off cleverly in that business. It is certain our Plumer did nothing to discountenance the rumor. He rather seemed pleased whenever it was, with all gentleness insinuated. But, besides his family pretensions, Plumer was an engaging fellow, and sang gloriously.—

Not so sweetly sang Plumer as thou sangest, mild, childlike, pastoral M——; a flute's breathing less divinely whispering than thy Arcadian melodies, when, in tones worthy of Arden, thou didst chant that song sung by Amiens to the banished duke, which proclaims the winter wind more lenient than for a man to be ungrateful. Thy sire was old surly M——, the unapproachable churchwarden of Bishopsgate. He knew not what he did, when he begat thee, like spring, gentle offspring of blustering winter: only unfortunate in thy ending, which should have been mild, conciliatory, swan-like.—

Much remains to sing. Many fantastic shapes rise up, but they must be mine in private—already I have fooled the reader to the top of his bent—else could I omit that strange creature Woollett, who existed in trying the question, and *bought litigations?*—and still stranger, inimitable, solemn Hepworth, from whose gravity Newton might have deduced the law of gravitation. How profoundly would he nib a pen—with what deliberation would he wet a wafer!—

But it is time to close—night's wheels are rattling fast over me—it is proper to have done with this solemn mockery.

Reader, what if I have been playing with thee all this while?—peradventure the very *names* which I have summoned up before thee are fantastic—unsubstantial—like Henry Pimpernel, and old John Naps of Greece.—

Be satisfied that something answering to them has had a being. Their importance is from the past.

OXFORD IN THE VACATION.

CASTING a preparatory glance at the bottom of this article—as the wary connoisseur in prints, with cursory eye (which, while it reads, seems as though it read not), never fails to consult the *quis sculpsit* in the corner, before he pronounces some rare piece to be a Vivares, or a Woollet—methinks I hear you exclaim, reader, *Who is Elia?*

Because in my last I tried to divert thee with some half-forgotten humors of some old clerks defunct, in an old house of business, long since gone to decay, doubtless, you have already set me down in your mind as one of the self-same college—a votary of the desk—a notched and cropped scrivener—one that sucks his sustenance, as certain sick people are said to do, through a quill.

Well, I do agnize something of the sort. I confess that it is my humor, my fancy—in the fore-part of the day, when the mind of your man of letters requires some relaxation—(and none better than such as at first sight seems most abhorrent from his beloved studies)—to while away some good hours of my time in the contemplation of indigos, cottons, raw silks, piece-goods, flowered or otherwise. In the first place . . . . and then it sends you home with such increased appetite to your books . . . . not to say, that your outside sheets, and waste

wrappers of foolscap, do receive into them, most kindly
and naturally, the impression of sonnets, epigrams, essays—so that the very parings of a counting-house are,
in some sort, the settings-up of an author. The enfran-
chised quill, that has plodded all the morning among
the cart-rucks of figures and ciphers, frisks and curvets
so at its ease over the flowery carpet-ground of a midnight dissertation. It feels its promotion. . . . So that
you see, upon the whole, the literary dignity of *Elia*
is very little, if at all, compromised in the condescen-
sion.

Not that, in my anxious detail of the many commodi-
ties incidental to the life of a public office, I would be
thought blind to certain flaws, which a cunning carper
might be able to pick in this Joseph's vest. And here I
must have leave, in the fullness of my soul, to regret the
abolition, and doing-away-with altogether, of those consolatory interstices, and sprinklings of freedom, through
the four seasons—the *red-letter days*, now become, to all
intents and purposes, *dead-letter days*. There was Paul,
and Stephen, and Barnabas—

"Andrew and John, men famous in old times"

—we were used to keep all their days holy, as long back
as I was at school at Christ's. I remember their effigies,
by the same token, in the old Basket Prayer-Book. There
hung Peter in his uneasy posture—holy Bartlemy in the
troublesome act of flaying, after the famous Marsyas by
Spagnoletti. I honored them all, and could almost have
wept the defalcation of Iscariot—so much did we love to
keep holy memories sacred—only methought I a little
grudged at the coalition of the *better Jude* with Simon—
clubbing (as it were) their sanctities together, to make

up one poor gaudy-day between them—as an economy unworthy of the dispensation.

These were bright visitations in a scholar's and a clerk's life—"far off their coming shone." I was as good as an almanac in those days. I could have told you such a saint's-day falls out next week, or the week after. Peradventure the Epiphany, by some periodical infelicity, would, once in six years, merge in a Sabbath. Now am I little better than one of the profane. Let me not be thought to arraign the wisdom of my civil superiors, who have judged the further observation of these holy tides to be papistical, superstitious. Only in a custom of such long standing, methinks, if their Holinesses the Bishops had, in decency, been first sounded—but I am wading out of my depths. I am not the man to decide the limits of civil and ecclesiastical authority—I am plain Elia—no Selden, nor Archbishop Usher—though at present in the thick of their books, here in the heart of learning, under the shadow of the mighty Bodley.

I can here play the gentleman, enact the student. To such a one as myself, who has been defrauded in his young years of the sweet food of academic institution, nowhere is so pleasant, to while away a few idle weeks at, as one or other of the Universities. Their vacation, too, at this time of the year, falls in so pat with *ours*. Here I can take my walks unmolested, and fancy myself of what degree or standing I please. I seem admitted *ad sundem*. I fetch up past opportunities. I can rise at the chapel-bell, and dream that it rings for *me*. In moods of humility I can be a Sizar, or a Servitor. When the peacock vein rises, I strut a Gentleman Commoner. In graver moments, I proceed Master of Arts. Indeed, I do not think I am much unlike that respectable character.

2

I have seen your dim-eyed vergers, and bed-makers in spectacles, drop a bow or a courtesy, as I pass, wisely mistaking me for something of the sort. I go about in black, which favors the notion. Only in Christ Church reverend quadrangle, I can be content to pass for nothing short of a Seraphic Doctor.

The walks at these times are so much one's own—the tall trees of Christ's, the groves of Magdalen! The halls deserted, and, with open doors, inviting one to slip in unperceived, and pay a devoir' to some Founder, or noble, or royal Benefactress (that should have been ours), whose portrait seems to smile upon their overlooked beadsman, and to adopt me for their own. Then, to take a peep in by the way at the butteries, and sculleries, redolent of antique hospitality: the immense caves of kitchens, kitchen fireplaces, cordial recesses; ovens whose first pies were baked four centuries ago; and spits which have cooked for Chaucer! Not the meanest minister among the dishes but is hallowed to me through his imagination, and the Cook goes forth a Manciple.

Antiquity! thou wondrous charm, what art thou? that, being nothing, art everything! When thou *wert*, thou wert not antiquity—then thou wert nothing, but hadst a remoter *antiquity*, as thou calledst it, to look back to with blind veneration; thou thyself being to thyself flat, jejune, *modern!* What mystery lurks in this retroversion? or what half Januses[1] are we, that cannot look forward with the same idolatry with which we forever revert! The mighty future is as nothing, being everything! the past is everything, being nothing!

---

[1] Januses of one face.—Sir Thomas Browne.

What were thy *dark ages?* Surely the sun rose as brightly then as now, and man got him to his work in the morning. Why is it we can never hear mention of them without an accompanying feeling, as though a palpable obscure had dimmed the face of things, and that our ancestors wandered to and fro groping!

Above all thy rarities, old Oxenford, what do most arride and solace me, are thy repositories of mouldering learning, thy shelves—

What a place to be in is an old library! It seems as though all the souls of all the writers, that have bequeathed their labors to these Bodleians, were reposing here, as in some dormitory, or middle state. I do not want to handle, to profane the leaves, their winding-sheets. I could as soon dislodge a shade. I seem to inhale learning, walking amid their foliage; and the odor of their old moth-scented coverings is fragrant as the first bloom of those sciential apples which grew amid the happy orchard.

Still less have I curiosity to disturb the elder repose of MSS. Those *variæ lectiones*, so tempting to the more erudite palates, do but disturb and unsettle my faith. I am no Herculanean raker. The credit of the three witnesses might have slept unimpeached for me. I leave these curiosities to Porson, and to G. D.—whom, by-the-way, I found busy as a moth over some rotten archive, rummaged out of some seldom-explored press, in a nook at Oriel. With long poring, he is grown almost into a book. He stood as passive as one by the side of the old shelves. I longed to new-coat him in russia, and assign him his place. He might have mustered for a tall Scapula.

D. is assiduous in his visits to these seats of learning.

No inconsiderate portion of his moderate fortune, I apprehend, is consumed in journeys between them and Clifford's Inn—where, like a dove on the asp's nest, he has long taken up his unconscious abode, amid an incongruous assembly of attorneys, attorneys' clerks, apparitors, promoters, vermin of the law, among whom he sits "in calm and sinless peace." The fangs of the law pierce him not; the winds of litigation blow over his humble chambers; the hard sheriff's officer moves his hat as he passes; legal nor illegal discourtesy touches him; none thinks of offering violence or injustice to him —you would as soon " strike an abstract idea."

D. has been engaged, he tells me, through a course of laborious years, in an investigation into all curious matter connected with the two Universities; and has lately lit upon a MS. collection of charters, relative to C——, by which he hopes to settle some disputed points—particularly that long controversy between them as to priority of foundation. The ardor with which he engages in these liberal pursuits, I am afraid, has not met with all the encouragement it deserved, either here or at C——. Your caputs and heads of colleges care less than anybody else about these questions. Contented to suck the milky fountains of their Alma Maters, without inquiring into the venerable gentlewomen's years, they rather hold such curiosities to be impertinent—unreverend. They have their good glebe-lands *in manu*, and care not much to rake into the title-deeds. I gather at least so much from other sources, for D. is not a man to complain.

D. started like un unbroke heifer when I interrupted him. *A priori* it was not very probable that we should have met in Oriel. But D. would have done the same had I accosted him on the sudden·in his own walks in Clifford's Inn, or in the Temple. In addition to a provoking short-sightedness (the effect of late studies and watchings at the midnight oil), D. is the most absent of men.· He made a call the other morning at our friend M.'s in Bedford Square; and, finding nobody at home, was ushered into the hall, where, asking for pen and ink, with great exactitude of purpose he enters me his name in the book—which ordinarily lies about in such places, to record the failures of the untimely or unfortunate visitor—and takes his leave with many ceremonies and professions of regret. Some two or three hours after, his walking destinies returned him into the same neighborhood again, and again the quiet image of the fireside circle at M.'s—Mrs. M. presiding at it like a Queen Lar, with pretty A. S. at her side—striking irresistibly on his fancy, he makes another call (forgetting that they were " certainly not to return from the country before that day week "), and, disappointed a second time, inquires for pen and paper as before; again the book is brought, and in the line just above that in which he is about to print his second name (his rescript)—his first name (scarce dry) looks out upon him like another Sosia, or as if a man should suddenly encounter his own duplicate! The effect may be conceived. D. made many a good resolution against any such lapses in the future. I hope he will not keep them too rigorously.

For with G. D., to be absent from the body is sometimes (not to speak it profanely) to be present with the Lord. At the very time when, personally encountering thee, he passes ·on with no recognition—or, being stopped, starts like a thing surprised—at that moment, reader, he is on Mount Tabor; or, Parnassus; or, co-

sphered with Plato ; or, with Harrington, framing " immortal Commonwealths," devising some plan of ameli-
oration to thy country or thy species—peradventure
meditating some individual kindness or courtesy, to be
done to *thee thyself*, the returning consciousness of
which made him to start so guiltily at thy obtruded personal presence.

D. is delightful anywhere, but he is at the best in
such places as these. He cares not much for Bath. He
is out of his element at Buxton, at Scarborough, or Har-
rowgate. The Oam and the Isis are to him "better than
all the waters of Damascus." On the Muses' hill he is
happy, and good, as one of the Shepherds on the Delec-
table Mountains; and when he goes about with you to
show you the halls and colleges, you think you have
with you the Interpreter of the House Beautiful.

CHRIST'S HOSPITAL FIVE–AND–THIRTY
YEARS AGO.

In Mr. Lamb's "Works," published a year or two
ago, I find a magnificent eulogy on my old school,* such
as it was, or now appears to him to have been, between
the years 1782 and 1789. It happens, very oddly, that
my own standing at Christ's was nearly corresponding
with his; and, with all gratitude to him for his enthusiasm for the cloisters, I think he has contrived to bring
together whatever can be said in praise of them, dropping all the other side of the argument most ingeniously.

* " Recollections of Christ's Hospital."

I remember L. at school; and can well recollect that
he had some peculiar advantages, which I and others of
his schoolfellows had not.   His friends lived in town,
and were near at hand; and he had the privilege of going to see them, almost as often as he wished, through
some invidious distinction, which was denied to us.   The
present worthy sub-treasurer to the Inner Temple can
explain how that happened.   He had his tea and hot
rolls in a morning, while we were battening upon our
quarter-of-a-penny loaf—our *crug*—moistened with attenuated small beer, in wooden piggings, smacking of
the pitched leathern jack it was poured from.   Our Mon-
day's milk-porridge, blue and tasteless, and the pease-
soup of Saturday, coarse and choking, were enriched for
him with a slice of "extraordinary bread and butter,"
from the hot-loaf of the Temple.   The Wednesday's mess
of millet, somewhat less repugnant—we had three ban-
yan to four meat days in the week—was endeared to his
palate with a lump of double-refined, and a smack of
ginger (to make it go down the more glibly) or the fragrant cinnamon.   In lieu of our *half-pickled* Sundays,
or *quite fresh* boiled beef on Thursdays (strong as *caro
equina*), with detestable marigolds floating in the pail to
poison the broth—our scanty mutton scrags on Fridays
—and rather more savory, but grudging, portions of the
same flesh, rotten-roasted or rare, on the Tuesdays (the
only dish which excited our appetites and disappointed
our stomachs in almost equal proportion)—he had his hot
plate of roast-veal, or the more tempting griskin (exotics
unknown to our palates), cooked in the paternal kitchen (a
great thing), and brought him daily by his maid or aunt!
I remember the good old relative (in whom love forbade
pride) squatted down upon some odd stone in a by-nook

of the cloisters, disclosing the viands (of higher regale
than those cates which the ravens ministered to the Tish-
bite); and the contending passions of L. at the unfolding. There was love for the bringer; shame for the
thing brought, and the manner of its bringing; sympathy for those who were too many to share in it; and, at
top of all, hunger (eldest, strongest of the passions!)
predominant, breaking down the stony fences of shame,
and awkwardness, and a troubling over-consciousness.

I was a poor, friendless boy. My parents, and those
who should care for me, were far away. Those few
acquaintances of theirs, which they could reckon upon
being kind to me in the great city, after a little forced
notice, which they had the grace to take of me on my
first arrival in town, soon grew tired of my holiday visits.
They seemed to them to recur too often, though I thought
them few enough; and, one after another, they all failed
me, and I felt myself alone among six hundred play-
mates.

Oh, the cruelty of separating a poor lad from his early
homestead! The yearnings which I used to have toward
it in those unfledged years! How, in my dreams, would
my native town (far in the west) come back, with its
church, and trees, and faces! How I would wake weeping, and in the anguish of my heart exclaim upon sweet
Calne in Wiltshire!

To this late hour of my life, I trace impressions left
by the recollection of those friendless holidays. The
long, warm days of summer never return but they bring
with them a gloom from the haunting memory of those
whole-day leaves, when, by some strange arrangement,
we were turned out for the live-long day upon our own
hands, whether we had friends to go to, or none. I

remember those bathing excursions to the New-River, which L. recalls with such relish, better, I think, than he can—for he was a home-seeking lad, and did not much care for such water pastimes:—How merrily we would sally forth into the fields; and strip under the first warmth of the sun; and wanton like young dace in the streams; getting us appetites for noon, which those of us that were penniless (our scanty morning crust long since exhausted) had not the means of allaying—while the cattle, and the birds, and the fishes, were at feed about us and we had nothing to satisfy our cravings—the very beauty of the day, and the exercise of the pastime, and the sense of liberty, setting a keener edge upon them!—How, faint and languid, finally, we would return, toward nightfall, to our desired morsel, half-rejoicing, half-reluctant, that the hours of our uneasy liberty had expired!

It was worse, in the days of winter, to go prowling about the streets objectless—shivering at cold windows of print-shops to extract a little amusement; or haply, as a last resort in hopes of a little novelty, to pay a fifty-times-repeated visit (where our individual faces should be as well known to the warden as those of his own charges) to the lions in the Tower—to whose levee, by courtesy, immemorial, we had a prescriptive title to admission.

L.'s governor (so we called the patron who presented us to the foundation) lived in a manner under his paternal roof. Any complaint which he had to make was sure of being attended to. This was understood at Christ's, and was an effectual screen to him against the severity of masters, or worse tyranny of the monitors. The oppressions of these young brutes are heart-sickening to call to recollection. I have been called out of my bed, and *waked for the purpose*, in the coldest winter nights —and this not once, but night after night—in my shirt, to receive the discipline of a leathern thong, with eleven other sufferers, because it pleased my callow overseer, when there has been any talking heard after we were gone to bed, to make the six last beds in the dormitory, where the youngest children of us slept, answerable for an offense they neither dared to commit, nor had the power to hinder. The same execrable tyranny drove the younger part of us from the fires, when our feet were perishing with snow ; and, under the cruelest penalties, forbade the indulgence of a drink of water, when we lay in sleepless summer nights, fevered with the season and the day's sports.

There was one H——, who, I learned in after-days, was seen expiating some maturer offense in the hulks. (Do I flatter myself in fancying that this might be the planter of that name, who suffered—at Nevis, I think, or St. Kitts—some few years since? My friend Tobin was the benevolent instrument of bringing him to the gallows.) This petty Nero actually branded a boy who had offended him, with a red-hot iron ; and nearly starved forty of us with exacting contributions, to the one-half of our bread, to pamper a young ass, which, incredible as it may seem, with the connivance of the nurse's daughter (a young flame of his), he had contrived to smuggle in, and keep upon the leads of the *ward*, as they called our dormitories. This game went on for better than a week, till the foolish beast, not able to fare well but he must cry roast-meat—happier than Caligula's minion, could he have kept his own counsel—but, foolisher, alas! than any of his species in the fables—waxing fat, and kicking, in the fullness of bread, one unlucky minute would needs proclaim his good fortune to the world below; and, laying out his simple throat, blew such a ram's-horn blast, as (toppling down the walls of his own Jericho) set concealment any longer at defiance. The client was dismissed, with certain attentions, to Smithfield; but I never understood that the patron underwent any censure on the occasion. This was in the stewardship of L.'s admired Perry.

Under the same *facile* administration can L. have forgotten the cool impunity with which the nurses used to carry away openly, in open platters, for their own tables, one out of two of every hot joint, which the careful matron had been seeing scrupulously weighed out for our dinners? These things were daily practised in that magnificent apartment, which L. (grown connoisseur since, we presume) praises so highly for the grand paintings "by Verrio and others," with which it is "hung round and adorned." But the sight of sleek, well-fed, blue-coat boys in the pictures was, at that time, I believe, little consolatory to him, or us, the living ones, who saw the better part of our provisions carried away before our faces by harpies; and ourselves reduced (with the Trojan in the hall of Dido)

"To feed our mind with idle portraiture."

L. has recorded the repugnance of the school to *gags*, or the fat of fresh beef boiled; and sets it down to some superstition. But these unctuous morsels are never grateful to young palates (children are universally fat-haters), and in strong, coarse, boiled meats, *unsalted*, are detestable. A *gag-eater* in our time was equivalent to a *goule*, and held in equal detestation—suffered under the imputation—

> —" 'T was said
> He ate strange flesh."

He was observed, after dinner, carefully to gather up the remnants left at his table (not many, nor very choice fragments, you may credit me)—and, in an especial manner, these disreputable morsels, which he would convey away, and secretly stow in the settle that stood at his bedside. None saw when he ate them. It was rumored that he privately devoured them in the night. He was watched, but no traces of such midnight practices were discoverable. Some reported that, on leave-days, he had been seen to carry out of the bounds a large blue check handkerchief full of something. This, then, must be the accursed thing. Conjecture next was at work to imagine how he could dispose of it. Some said he sold it to the beggars. This belief generally prevailed. He went about moping. None spake to him. No one would play with him. He was excommunicated; put out of the pale of the school. He was too powerful a boy to be beaten, but he underwent every mode of that negative punishment which is more grievous than many stripes. Still he persevered. At length he was observed by two of his school-fellows, who were determined to get at the secret, and had traced him one leave-day for that purpose, to enter a large, worn-out building, such as there exist specimens of in Chancery Lane, which are let out to various scales of pauperism, with open door and a common staircase. After him they silently slunk in, and followed by stealth up four flights, and saw him tap at a poor wicket, which was opened by an aged woman, meanly clad. Suspicion was now r'pened into certainty.

The informers had secured their victim. They had him
in their toils. Accusation was formally preferred, and
retribution most signal was looked for. Mr. Hathaway,
the then steward (for this happened a little after my
time), with that patient sagacity which tempered all his
conduct, determined to investigate the matter before he
proceeded to sentence. The result was that the supposed
mendicants, the receivers or purchasers of the mysterious scraps, turned out to be the parents of ——, an honest couple come to decay—whom this seasonable supply
had, in all probability, saved from mendicancy; and this
young stork, at the expense of his own good name, had
all this while been only feeding the old birds!—The governors on this occasion, much to their honor, voted a
present relief to the family of ——, and presented him
with a silver medal. The lesson which the steward read
upon RASH JUDGMENT, on the occasion of publicly deliver-
ing the medal to ——, I believe would not be lost upon
his auditory.—I had left school then, but I well remember ——. He was a tall, shambling youth, with a cast
in his eye, not at all calculated to conciliate hostile prejudices. I have since seen him carrying a baker's basket.
I think I heard he did not do quite so well by himself, as
he had done by the old folks.

I was an hypochondriac lad; and the sight of a boy
in fetters, upon the day of my first putting on the blue
clothes, was not exactly fitted to assuage the natural terrors of initiation. I was of tender years, barely turned
of seven; and had only read of such things in book, or
seen them but in dreams. I was told he had *run away*.
This was the punishment for the first offense. As a novice
I was soon after taken to see the dungeons. These were
little, square Bedlam cells, where a boy could just lie at

his length upon straw, and a blanket—a mattress, I think, was afterward substituted—with a peep of light, let in askance, from a prison orifice at top, barely enough to read by. Here the poor boy was locked in by himself all day, without sight of any but the porter who brought him his bread and water—who *might not speak to him;* —or of the beadle, who came twice a week to call him out to receive his periodical chastisement, which was almost welcome, because it separated him for a brief interval from solitude: and here he was shut up by himself *of nights* out of the reach of any sound, to suffer whatever horrors the weak nerves, and superstition incident to his time of life, might subject him to.* This was the penalty for the second offense. Wouldst thou like, reader, to see what became of him in the next degree?

The culprit, who had been a third time an offender, and whose expulsion was at this time deemed irreversible, was brought forth, as at some solemn *auto-da-fé*, arrayed in uncouth and most appalling attire—all trace of his late "watchet weeds" carefully effaced, he was exposed in a jacket resembling those which London lamplighters formerly delighted in, with a cap of the same. The effect of this divestiture was such as the ingenious devisers of it could have anticipated. With his pale and frighted features, it was as if some of those disfigurements in Dante had seized upon him. In this disguisement he was brought into the hall (*L.'s favorite state-*

---

* One or two instances of lunacy, or attempted suicide, accordingly, at length convinced the governors of the impolicy of this part of the sentence, and the midnight torture to the spirits was dispensed with.—This fancy of dungeons for children was a sprout of Howard's brain; for which (saving the reverence due to Holy Paul), methinks, I could willingly spit upon his statue.

room), where awaited him the whole number of his school-fellows, whose joint lessons and sports he was thenceforth to share no more; the awful presence of the steward, to be seen for the last time; of the executioner beadle, clad in his state-robe for the occasion; and of two faces more, of direr import, because never but in these extremities visible. These were governors: two of whom by choice, or charter, were always accustomed to officiate at these *Ultima Supplicia;* not to mitigate (so at least we understood it), but to enforce the utter-most stripe. Old Bamber Gascoigne, and Peter Aubert, I remember, were colleagues on one occasion, when the beadle turning rather pale, a glass of brandy was ordered to prepare him for the mysteries. The scourging was, after the old Roman fashion, long and stately. The lictor accompanied the criminal quite round the hall. We were generally too faint with attending to the previous disgust-ing circumstances, to make accurate report with our eyes of the degree of corporal suffering inflicted. Report, of course, gave out the back knotty and livid. After scourg-ing, he was made over, in his *San Benito*, to his friends, if he had any (but commonly such poor runagates were friendless), or to his parish officer, who, to enhance the effect of the scene, had his station allotted to him on the outside of the hall-gate.

These solemn pageantries were not played off so often as to spoil the general mirth of the community. We had plenty of exercise and recreation *after* school-hours; and, for myself, I must confess, that I was never happier than *in* them. The Upper and the Lower Grammar-Schools were held in the same room; and an imaginary line only divided their bounds. Their character was as different as that of the inhabitants on the two sides of the Pyrenees. The Rev. James Boyer was the Upper Master; but the Rev. Matthew Field presided over that portion of the apartment of which I had the good fortune to be a member. We lived a life as careless as birds. We talked and did just what we pleased, and nobody molested us. We carried an accidence, or a grammar, for form; but, for any trouble it gave us, we might take two years in getting through the verbs deponent, and another two in forgeting all that we had learned about them. There was now and then the formality of saying a lesson, but if you had not learned it, a brush across the shoulders (just enough to disturb a fly) was the sole remonstrance. Field never used the rod; and in truth he wielded the cane with no great good-will—holding it "like a dancer." It looked in his hands rather like an emblem than an instrument of authority; and an emblem, too, he was ashamed of. He was a good, easy man, that did not care to ruffle his own peace, nor perhaps set any great consideration upon the value of juvenile time. He came among us, now and then, but often staid away whole days from us; and when he came it made no difference to us—he had his private room to retire to, the short time he staid, to be out of the sound of our noise. Our mirth and uproar went on. We had classics of our own, without being beholden to "insolent Greece or haughty Rome," that passed current among us—Peter Wilkins— the Adventures of the Hon. Captain Robert Boyle—the Fortunate Blue-Coat Boy—and the like. Or we cultivated a turn for mechanic and scientific operations; making little sun-dials of paper; or weaving those ingenious parentheses called cat-cradles; or making dry peas to dance upon the end of a tin pipe; or studying the art military over that laudable game "French and English," and a hundred other such devices to pass away the time —mixing the useful with the agreeable—as would have made the souls of Rousseau and John Locke chuckle to have seen us.

Matthew Field belonged to that class of modest divines who affect to mix in equal proportion the *gentleman*, the *scholar*, and the *Christian;* but, I know not how, the first ingredient is generally found to be the predominating dose in the composition. He was engaged in gay parties, or with his courtly bow at some episcopal levee, when he should have been attending upon us. He had for many years the classical charge of a hundred children, during the four or five first years of their education; and his very highest form seldom proceeded further than two or three of the introductory fables of Phædrus. How things were suffered to go on thus, I cannot guess. Boyer, who was the proper person to have remedied these abuses, always affected, perhaps felt, a delicacy in interfering in a province not strictly his own. I have not been without my suspicions that he was not altogether displeased at the contrast we presented to his end of the school. We were a sort of Helots to his young Spartans. He would sometimes, with ironic deference, send to borrow a rod of the Under Master, and then, with Sardonic grin, observe to one of his upper boys "how neat and fresh the twigs looked." While his pale students were battering their brains over Xenophon and Plato, with a silence as deep as that enjoined by the Samite, we were enjoying ourselves at our ease in our little Goshen. We saw a little into the secrets of his discipline, and the prospect did but the more reconcile us to our lot. His thunders rolled innocuous for us; his storms came near, but never touched us;

3

contrary to Gideon's miracle, while all around were
drenched, our fleece was dry.* His boys turned out the
better scholars; we, I suspect, have the advantage in
temper. His pupils cannot speak of him without something of terror allaying their gratitude; the remembrance of Field comes back with all the soothing images
of indolence, and summer slumbers, and work like play,
and innocent idleness, and Elysian exemptions, and life
itself a "playing holiday."

Though sufficiently removed from the jurisdiction of
Boyer, we were near enough (as I have said) to understand a little of his system. We occasionally heard
sounds of the *Ululantes*, and caught glances of Tartarus.
B. was a rabid pedant. His English style was cramped
to barbarism. His Easter anthems (for his duty obliged
him to those periodical flights) were grating as scrannel
pipes.† He would laugh, ay, and heartily, but then it
must be at Flaccus's quibble about *Rex*—or at the *tristis
severitas in vultu*, or *inspicere in patinas*, of Terence—
thin jests, which at their first broaching could hardly
have had *vis* enough to move a Roman muscle. He had
two wigs, both pedantic, but of different omen. The
one serene, smiling, fresh-powdered, betokening a mild
day. The other, an old, discolored, unkempt, angry

---

* Cowley.

† In this and everything B. was the antipodes of his coadju-
tor. While the former was digging his brains for crude anthems,
worth a pig-nut, F. would be recreating his gentlemanly fancy
in the more flowery walks of the Muses. A little dramatic effu-
sion of his, under the name of Vertumnus and Pomona, is not
yet forgotten by the chroniclers of that sort of literature. It
was accepted by Garrick, but the town did not give it their sanc-
tion. B. used to say of it, in a way of half compliment, half
irony, that it was *too classical for representation*.

caxon, denoting frequent and bloody execution. Woe
to the school when he made his morning appearance in
his *passy*, or *passionate wig!* No comet expounded
surer. J. B. had a heavy hand. I have known him
double his knotty fist at a poor, trembling child (the maternal milk hardly dry upon its lips), with a "Sirrah, do
you presume to set your wits at me?" Nothing was
more common than to see him make a headlong entry
into the school-room, from his inner recess or library,
and, with turbulent eye, singling out a lad, roar out,
"Od's my life, sirrah" (his favorite adjuration), "I have
a great mind to whip you;" then, with as sudden a re-
tracting impulse, fling back into his lair, and, after a
cooling lapse of some minutes (during which all but the
culprit had totally forgotten the context) drive headlong
out again, piecing out his imperfect sense, as if it had
been some Devil's Litany, with the expletory yell—"*and
I* WILL, *too.*" In his gentler moods, when the *rabidus
furor* was assuaged, he had resort to an ingenious
method, peculiar, for what I have heard, to himself, of
whipping the boy, and reading the Debates, at the same
time; a paragraph, and a lash between; which in those
times, when parliamentary oratory was most at a height
and flourishing in these realms, was not calculated to
impress the patient with a veneration for the diffuser
graces of rhetoric.

Once, and but once, the uplifted rod was known to
fall ineffectual from his hand—when droll, squinting W.,
having been caught putting the inside of the master's
desk to a use for which the architect had clearly not
designed it, to justify himself, with great simplicity
averred that *he did not know that the thing had been
forewarned.* This exquisite irrecognition of any law

antecedent to the *oral* or *declaratory*, struck so irresistibly upon the fancy of all who heard it (the pedagogue himself not excepted) that remission was unavoidable.

L. has given credit to B.'s great merits as an instructor. Coleridge, in his literary life, has pronounced a more intelligible and ample encomium on them. The author of the *Country Spectator* doubts not to compare him with the ablest teachers of antiquity. Perhaps we cannot dismiss him better than with the pious ejaculation of C., when he heard that his old master was on his death-bed: "Poor J. B.! may all his faults be forgiven; and may he be wafted to bliss by little cherub-boys all head and wings, with no *bottoms* to reproach his sublunary infirmities."

Under him were many good and sound scholars bred. First Grecian of my time was Lancelot Pepys Stevens, kindest of boys and men, since Co-grammar-master (and inseparable companion) with Dr. T——e. What an edifying spectacle did this brace of friends present to those who remembered the anti-socialities of their predecessors! You never met the one by chance in the street without a wonder, which was quickly dissipated by the almost immediate sub-appearance of the other. Generally arm-in-arm, these kindly coadjutors lightened for each other the toilsome duties of their profession, and when, in advanced age, one found it convenient to retire, the other was not long in discovering that it suited him to lay down the fasces also. Oh, it is pleasant, as it is rare, to find the same arm linked in yours at forty, which at thirteen helped it to turn over the *Cicero de Amicitiâ*, or some tale of Antique Friendship, which the young heart even then was burning to anticipate! Co-Grecian with S. was Th——, who has since executed

with ability various diplomatic functions at the Northern
courts. Th—— was a tall, dark, saturnine youth, spar-
ing of speech, with raven looks. Thomas Fanshaw Mid-
dleton followed him (now Bishop of Calcutta), a scholar
and a gentleman in his teens. He has the reputation of
an excellent critic; and is author (besides the *Country
Spectator*) of a Treatise on the Greek Article, against
Sharpe. M. is said to bear his mitre high in India,
where the *regni novitas* (I dare say) sufficiently justifies
the bearing. A humility quite as primitive as that of
Jewel or Hooker might not be exactly fitted to impress
the minds of those Anglo-Asiatic diocesans with a reverence for home institutions, and the Church which those
fathers watered. The manners of M. at school, though
firm, were mild and unassuming. Next to M. (if not
senior to him) was Richards, author of the Aboriginal
Britons, the most spirited of the Oxford Prize Poems;
a pale, studious Grecian. Then followed poor S——,
ill-fated M——! of these the Muse is silent.

> " Finding some of Edward's race
> Unhappy, pass their annals by."

Come back into memory, like as thou wert in the
day-spring of thy fancies, with hope like a fiery column
before thee—the dark pillar not yet turned —Samuel
Taylor Coleridge—Logician, Metaphysician, Bard!—How
have I seen the casual passer through the Cloisters stand
still, entranced with admiration (while he weighed the dis-
proportion between the *speech* and the *garb* of the young
Mirandula), to hear thee unfold, in thy deep and sweet
intonations, the mysteries of Jamblichus or Plotinus (for
even in those years thou waxedst not pale at such philo-
sophic draughts), or reciting Homer in his Greek, or

Pindar—while the walls of the old Grey Friars reëchoed
to the accents of the *inspired charity-boy !*—Many were
the " wit-combats " (to dally awhile with the words of
old Fuller) between him and O. V. Le G——, "which
two I behold like a Spanish great galleon and an English
man-of-war ; Master Coleridge, like the former, was
built far higher in learning, solid, but slow in his performances.   O. V. L., with the English man-of-war,
lesser in bulk, but lighter in sailing, could turn with all
tides, tack about, and take advantage of all winds, by
the quickness of his wit and invention."

Nor shalt thou, their compeer, be quickly forgotten,
Allen, with the cordial smile, and still more cordial
laugh, with which thou wert wont to make the old
Cloisters shake, in thy cognition of some poignant jest
of theirs; or the anticipation of some more material,
and, peradventure, practical one, of thine own.   Extinct
are those smiles, with that beautiful countenance, with
which (for thou wert the *Nireus formosus* of the school),
in the days of thy maturer waggery, thou didst disarm
the wrath of infuriated town damsel, who, incensed by
provoking pinch, turning tigress-like round, suddenly
converted by thy angel-look, exchanged the half-formed
terrible " *bl—*," for a gentler greeting—" *bless thy handsome face !* "

Next follow two, who ought to be now alive, and the
friends of Elia—the junior Le G—— and F——, who,
impelled, the former by a roving temper, the latter by
too quick a sense of neglect, ill capable of enduring the
slights poor Sizars are sometimes subject to in our seats
of learning, exchanged their Alma Mater for the camp ;
perishing, one by climate, and one on the plains of Sal-
amanca: Le G——, sanguine, volatile, sweet-natured ;

F——, dogged, faithful, anticipative of insult, warm-hearted, with something of the old Roman height about him.

Fine, frank-hearted Fr——, the present master of Hertford, with Marmaduke T——, mildest of Missionaries—and both my good friends still—close the catalogue of Grecians in my time. ·

THE TWO RACES OF MEN.

THE human species, according to the best theory I can form of it, is composed of two distinct races, *the men who borrow, and the men who lend.* To these two original diversities may be reduced all those impertinent classifications of Gothic and Celtic tribes, white men, black men, red men. All the dwellers upon earth, "Parthians, and Medes, and Elamites," flock hither, and do naturally fall in with one or other of these primary distinctions. The infinite superiority of the former, which I choose to designate as the *great race,* is discernible in their figure, port, and a certain instinctive sovereignty. The latter are born degraded. "He shall serve his brethren." There is something in the air of one of this cast, lean and suspicious; contrasting with the open, trusting, generous manners of the other.

Observe who have been the greatest borrowers of all ages—Alcibiades, Falstaff, Sir Richard Steele, our late incomparable Brinsley—what a family likeness in all four !

What a careless, even deportment hath your borrower! what rosy gills! what a beautiful reliance on Provi-

dence doth he manifest, taking no more thought than
lilies! What contempt for money, accounting it (yours
and mine especially) no better than dross! What a liberal confounding of those pedantic distinctions of *meum*
and *tuum*! or rather, what a noble simplification of language (beyond Tooke), resolving these supposed oppo-
sites into one clear, intelligible pronoun adjective!—
What near approaches doth he make to the primitive
community, to the extent of one-half of the principle at
least!

He is the true taxer who "calleth all the world up to
be taxed;" and the distance is as vast between him and
one of us, as subsisted between the Augustan Majesty
and the poorest obolary Jew that paid it tribute-pittance
at Jerusalem!—His exactions, too, have such a cheerful,
voluntary air! So far removed from your sour parochial or state-gatherers, those ink-horn varlets, who
carry their want of welcome in their faces! He com-
eth to you with a smile, and troubleth you with no re-
ceipt; confining himself to no set season. Every day is
his Candlemas, or his Feast of Holy Michael. He ap-
plieth the *lene tormentum* of a pleasant look to your
purse—which to that gentle warmth expands her silken
leaves, as naturally as the cloak of the traveler, for which
sun and wind contended! He is the true Propontic
which never ebbeth! The sea which taketh handsomely
at each man's hand. In vain the victim, whom he de-
lighteth to honor, struggles with destiny; he is in the
net. Lend therefore cheerfully, O man ordained to lend
—that thou lose not in the end, with thy worldly penny,
the reversion promised. Combine not preposterously in
thine own person the penalties of Lazarus and of Dives!
but when thou seest the proper authority coming, meet

it smilingly, as it were half-way. Come, a handsome
sacrifice! See how light *he* makes of it! Strain not
courtesies with a noble enemy.

Reflections like the foregoing were forced upon my
mind by the death of my old friend Ralph Bigod, Esq.,
who parted this life, on Wednesday evening, dying, as
he had lived, without much trouble. He boasted himself a descendant from mighty ancestors of that name,
who heretofore held ducal dignities in this realm. In
his actions and sentiments he belied not the stock to
which he pretended. Early in life he found himself invested with ample revenues; which, with that noble dis-
interestedness which I have noticed as inherent in men
of the *great race*, he took almost immediate measures
entirely to dissipate and bring to nothing: for there is
something revolting in the idea of a king holding a private purse, and the thoughts of Bigod were all regal.
Thus furnished by the very act of disfurnishment; getting rid of the cumbersome luggage of riches, more apt
(as one sings)

> "To slacken virtue, and abate her edge,
>   Than prompt her to do aught may merit praise,"

he set forth, like some Alexander, upon his great enter-
prise, "borrowing and to borrow!"

In his periegesis, or triumphant progress throughout
this island, it has been calculated that he laid a tithe
part of the inhabitants under contribution. I reject this
estimate as greatly exaggerated: but having had the
honor of accompanying my friend divers times, in his
perambulations about this vast city, I own I was greatly
struck at first with the prodigious number of faces we
met, who claimed a sort of respectful acquaintance with

us. He was one day so obliging as to explain the phenomenon. It seems, these were his tributaries; feeders of his exchequer; gentlemen, his good friends (as he was pleased to express himself), to whom he had occasionally been beholden for a loan. Their multitudes did no way disconcert him. He rather took a pride in numbering them; and, with Comus, seemed pleased to be "stocked with so fair a herd."

With such sources, it was a wonder how he contrived to keep his treasury always empty. He did it by force of an aphorism, which he had often in his mouth, that "money kept longer than three days stinks." So he made use of it while it was fresh. A good part he drank away (for he was an excellent toss-pot); some he gave away, the rest he threw away, literally tossing and hurling it violently from him—as boys do burs, or as if it had been infectious—into ponds, or ditches, or deep holes, inscrutable cavities of the earth; or he would bury it (where he would never seek it again) by a river's side under some bank, which (he would facetiously observe) paid no interest—but outway from him it must go peremptorily, as Hagar's offspring into the wilderness, while it was sweet. He never missed it. The streams were perennial which fed his fisc. When new supplies became necessary, the first person that had the felicity to fall in with him, friend or stranger, was sure to contribute to the deficiency. For Bigod had an *undeniable* way with him. He had a cheerful, open exterior, a quick, jovial eye, a bald forehead, just touched with gray (*cana fides*). He anticipated no excuse, and found none. And, waiving for a while my theory as to the *great race*, I would put it to the most untheorizing reader, who may at times have disposable coin in his pocket, whether it is not more repugnant to the kindliness of his nature to refuse such a one as I am describing, than to say *no* to a poor petitionary rogue (your bastard borrower), who, by his mumping visnomy, tells you that he expects nothing better; and, therefore, whose preconceived notions and expectations you do in reality so much less shock in the refusal.

When I think of this man; his fiery glow of heart; his swell of feeling; how magnificent, how *ideal* he was; how great at the midnight hour; and when I compare with him the companions with whom I have associated since, I grudge the saving of a few idle ducats, and think that I am fallen into the society of *lenders* and *little* men.

To one like Elia, whose treasures are rather cased in leather covers than closed in iron coffers, there is a class of alienators more formidable than that which I have touched upon; I mean your *borrowers of books*—those mutilators of collections, spoilers of the symmetry of shelves, and creators of odd volumes. There is Comberbatch, matchless in his depredations!

That foul gap in the bottom shelf facing you, like a great eye-tooth knocked out—(you are now with me in my little back study in Bloomsbury, reader!)—with the huge Switzer-like tomes on each side (like the Guildhall giants, in their reformed posture, guardant of nothing), once held the tallest of my folios, *Opera Bonaventuræ*, choice and massy divinity, to which its two supporters (school divinity also, but of a lesser calibre—Bellarmine, and Holy Thomas) showed but as dwarfs—itself an Ascapart!—*that* Comberbatch abstracted upon the faith of a theory he holds, which is more easy, I confess, for me to suffer by than to refute, namely, that "the title

to property in a book (my Bonaventura, for instance) is
in exact ratio to the claimant's powers of understanding
and appreciating the same." Should he go on acting
upon this theory, which of our shelves is safe?

The slight vacuum in the left-hand case—two shelves
from the ceiling—scarcely distinguishable but by the
quick eye of a loser—was whilom the commodious resting-place of Brown on Urn Burial. C. will hardly al-
lege that he knows more about that treatise than I do,
who introduced it to him, and was, indeed, the first (of
the moderns) to discover its beauties—but so have I
known a foolish lover to praise his mistress in the presence of a rival more qualified to carry her off than himself. Just below, Dodsley's dramas want their fourth volume, where Vittoria Corombona is! The remainder
nine are as distasteful as Priam's refuse sons, when the
Fates *borrowed* Hector. Here stood the Anatomy of
Melancholy, in sober state. There loitered the Complete
Angler; quiet as in life, by some stream-side. In yonder
nook, John Buncle, a widower - volume, with "eyes
closed," mourns his ravished mate.

One justice I must do my friend, that if he sometimes,
like the sea, sweeps away a treasure, at another time,
sea-like, he throws up as rich an equivalent to match it.
I have a small under-collection of this nature (my friend's
gatherings in his various calls), picked up, he has forgotten at what odd places, and deposited with as little memory at mine. I take in these orphans, the twice deserted.
These proselytes of the gate are welcome as the true He-
brews. There they stand in conjunction; natives and
naturalized. The latter seem as little disposed to inquire
out their true lineage as I am.—I charge no warehouse-
room for these deodands, nor shall ever put myself to

the ungentlemanly trouble of advertising a sale of them
to pay expenses.

To lose a volume to C. carries some sense and meaning in it. You are sure that he will make one hearty
meal on your viands, if he can give no account of the
platter after it. But what moved thee, wayward, spiteful K., to be so importunate to carry off with thee, in
spite of tears and adjurations to thee to forbear, the
Letters of that princely woman, the thrice noble Margaret Newcastle?—knowing at the time, and knowing
that I knew, also, thou most assuredly wouldst never
turn over one leaf of the illustrious folio—what but the
mere spirit of contradiction, and childish love of getting
the better of thy friend?—Then, worst cut of all! to
transport it with thee to the Gallican land—

"Unworthy land to harbor such a sweetness,
  A virtue in which all ennobling thoughts dwelt,
  Pure thoughts, kind thoughts, high thoughts, her sex's wonder!"

—hadst thou not thy play-books, and books of jests and
fancies, about thee, to keep thee merry, even as thou
keepest all companies with thy quips and mirthful tales?
Child of the green-room, it was unkindly done of thee.
Thy wife, too, that part-French, better-part English-
woman!—that *she* could fix upon no other treatise to
bear away, in kindly token of remembering us, than the
works of Fulke Greville, Lord Brook — of which no
Frenchman, nor woman of France, Italy, or England,
was ever by nature constituted to comprehend a tittle!—
Was there not Zimmermann on Solitude?

Reader, if haply thou art blessed with a moderate
collection, be shy of showing it; or if thy heart over-
floweth to lend them, lend thy books; but let it be to

such a one as S. T. C.—he will return them (generally
anticipating the time appointed) with usury; enriched
with annotations tripling their value. I have had experience. Many of these precious MSS. of his—(in *matter*
oftentimes, and almost in *quantity* not unfrequently,
vying with the originals) in no very clerkly hand—legi-
ble in my Daniel; in old Burton; in Sir Thomas Browne;
and those abstruser cogitations of the Greville, now,
alas! wandering in Pagan lands.—I counsel thee, shut
not thy heart, nor thy library, against S. T. C.

NEW-YEAR'S-EVE.

EVERY man hath two birthdays; two days, at least,
in every year, which set him upon revolving the lapse of
time, as it affects his mortal duration. The one is that
which in an especial manner he termeth *his*. In the
gradual desuetude of old observances, this custom of
solemnizing our proper birthday hath nearly passed
away, or is left to children, who reflect nothing at all
about the matter, nor understand anything in it beyond
cake and orange. But the birth of a New Year is of an
interest too wide to be pretermitted by king or cobbler.
No one ever regarded the first of January with indifference. It is that from which all date their time, and
count upon what is left. It is the nativity of our common Adam.

Of all sound of all bells—bells, the music nighest
bordering upon heaven—most solemn and touching is
the peal which rings out the Old Year. I never heard
it without a gathering-up of my mind to a concentration

of all the images that have been diffused over the past twelvemonth; all I have done or suffered, performed or neglected, in that regretted time. I begin to know its worth, as when a person dies. It takes a personal color; nor was it a poetical flight in a contemporary when he exclaimed—

"I saw the skirts of the departing year."

It is no more than what, in sober sadness, every one of us seems to be conscious of, in that awful leave-taking. I am sure I felt it, and all felt it with me, last night; though some of my companions affected rather to manifest an exhilaration at the birth of the coming year, than any very tender regrets for the decease of its predecessor. But I am none of those who—

"Welcome the coming, speed the parting guest."

I am naturally, beforehand, shy of novelties: new books, new faces, new years—from some mental twist which makes it difficult in me to face the prospective. I have almost ceased to hope; and am sanguine only in the prospects of other (former) years. I plunge into foregone visions and conclusions. I encounter pell-mell with past disappointments. I am armor-proof against old discouragements. I forgive, or overcome in fancy, old adversaries. I play over again *for love*, as the gamesters phrase it, games for which I once paid so dear. I would scarce now have any of those untoward accidents and events of my life reversed. I would no more alter them than the incidents of some well-contrived novel. Methinks it is better that I should have pined away seven of my goldenest years, when I was thrall to the fair hair and fairer eyes of Alice W—n, than that so passion-

ate a love-adventure should be lost. It was better that
our family should have missed that legacy which old
Dorrell cheated us of, than that I should have at this
moment two thousand pounds *in banco*, and be without
the idea of that specious old rogue.

In a degree beneath manhood, it is my infirmity to
look back upon those early days. Do I advance a paradox when I say that, skipping over the intervention of
forty years, a man may have leave to love *himself*, without the imputation of self-love?

If I know aught of myself, no one whose mind is in-
trospective—and mine is painfully so—can have a less
respect for his present identity than I have for the man
Elia. I know him to be light and vain and humorsome;
a notorious —— ; addicted to —— ; averse from counsel, neither taking it nor offering it ; —— besides ; a
stammering buffoon—what you will, lay it on and spare
not: I subscribe to it all, and much more than thou
canst be willing to lay at his door; but for the child
Elia, that "other me" there in the background, I must
take leave to cherish the remembrance of that young
master, with as little reference, I protest, to this stupid
changeling of five-and-forty as if it had been a child of
some other house and not of my parents. I can cry over
its patient small-pox at five and rougher mendicaments.
I can lay its poor fevered head upon the sick-pillow at
Christ's, and wake with it in surprise at the gentle posture of maternal tenderness hanging over it, that unknown had watched its sleep. I know how it shrank
from any the least color of falsehood. God help thee,
Elia, how art thou changed! Thou art sophisticated.
I know how honest, how courageous (for a weakling),
it was—how religious, how imaginative, how hopeful!

From what have I not fallen, if the child I remember
was indeed myself—and not some dissembling guardian
presenting a false identity to give the rule to my un-
practised steps and regulate the tone of my moral being!

That I am fond of indulging, beyond a hope of sympathy, in such retrospection, may be the symptom of
some sickly idiosyncrasy. Or, is it owing to another
cause: simply that, being without wife or family, I have
not learned to project myself enough out of myself;
and, having no offspring of my own to dally with, I
turn back upon memory, and adopt my own early idea
as my heir and favorite? If these speculations seem
fantastical to thee, reader (a busy man, perchance), if I
tread out of the way of thy sympathy, and am singular-
ly conceited only, I retire, impenetrable to ridicule, under the phantom-cloud of Elia.

The elders, with whom I was brought up, were of a
character not likely to let slip the sacred observance of
any old institution: and the ringing out of the old year
was kept by them with circumstances of peculiar ceremony.—In those days the sound of those midnight
chimes, though it seemed to raise hilarity in all around
me, never failed to bring a train of pensive imagery
into my fancy. Yet I then scarce conceived what it
meant, or thought of it as a reckoning that concerned
me. Not childhood alone, but the young man till thirty,
never feels practically that he is mortal. He knows it,
indeed, and, if need were, he could preach a homily on
the fragility of life; but he brings it not home to himself, any more than in a hot June we can appropriate to
our imagination the freezing days of December. But
now—shall I confess a truth?—I feel these audits but
too powerfully. I begin to count the probabilities of

4

my duration, and to grudge at the expenditure of moments and shortest periods, like misers' farthings. In proportion as the years both lessen and shorten, I set more count upon their periods, and would fain lay my ineffectual finger upon the spoke of the great wheel. I am not content to pass away "like a weaver's shuttle." Those metaphors solace me not, nor sweeten the unpalatable draught of mortality. I care not to be carried with the tide, that smoothly bears human life to eternity; and reluct at the inevitable course of destiny. I am in love with this green earth, the face of town and country, the unspeakable rural solitudes, and the sweet security of streets. I would set up my tabernacle here. I am content to stand still at the age to which I am arrived, I and my friends, to be no younger, no richer, no handsomer. I do not want to be weaned by age, or drop, like mellow fruit, as they say, into the grave.— Any alteration, on this earth of mine, in diet or in lodging, puzzles and discomposes me. My household gods plant a terrible fixed foot, and are not rooted up without blood. They do not willingly seek Lavinian shores. A new state of being staggers me.

Sun, and sky, and breeze, and solitary walks, and summer holidays, and the greenness of fields, and the delicious juices of meats and fishes, and society, and the cheerful glass, and candle-light, and fireside conversations, and innocent vanities and jests, and *irony itself*— do these things go out with life?

Can a ghost laugh or shake his gaunt sides, when you are pleasant with him?

And you, my midnight darlings, my Folios! must I part with the intense delight of having you (huge armfuls) in my embraces? Must knowledge come to me, if

it come at all, by some awkward experiment of in-
tuition, and no longer by this familiar process of reading?

Shall I enjoy friendships there, wanting the smiling
indications which point me to them here—the recogniza-
ble face—the "sweet assurance of a look"—?

In winter this intolerable disinclination to dying—to
give it its mildest name—does more especially haunt and
beset me. In a genial August noon, beneath a swelter-
ing sky, death is almost problematic. At those times do
such poor snakes as myself enjoy an immortality. Then
we expand and burgeon. Then we are as strong again,
as valiant again, as wise again, and a great deal taller.
The blast that nips and shrinks me, puts me in thoughts
of death. All things allied to the insubstantial, wait upon
that master-feeling; cold, numbness, dreams, perplexity;
moonlight itself, with its shadowy and spectral appearances—that cold ghost of the sun, or Phœbus's sickly
sister, like that innutritious one denounced in the Canti-
cles—I am none of her minions—I hold with the Persian.

. Whatever thwarts, or puts me out of my way, brings
death into my mind. All partial evils, like humors, run
into that capital plague-sore.—I have heard some profess
an indifference to life. Such hail the end of their existence as a port of refuge; and speak of the grave as of
some soft arms, in which they may slumber as on a pillow. Some have wooed death—but out upon thee, I say,
thou foul, ugly phantom! I detest, abhor, execrate, and
(with Friar John) give thee to sixscore thousand devils,
as in no instance to be excused or tolerated, but shunned
as a universal viper; to be branded, proscribed, and
spoken evil of! In no way can I be brought to digest

thee, thou thin, melancholy *Privation*, or more frightful
and confounding *Positive!*

Those antidotes, prescribed against the fear of thee,
are altogether frigid and insulting, like thyself. For
what satisfaction hath a man, that he shall "lie down
with kings and emperors in death," who in his lifetime
never greatly coveted the society of such bedfellows?—
or, forsooth, that "so shall the fairest face appear?"—
why, to comfort me, must Alice W——n be a goblin?
More than all, I conceive disgust at those impertinent
and misbecoming familiarities, inscribed upon your ordinary tombstones. Every dead man must take upon himself to be lecturing me with his odious truism, that
"Such as he now is I must shortly be." Not so shortly,
friend, perhaps as thou imaginest. In the mean time I
am alive. I move about. I am worth twenty of thee.
Know thy betters! Thy New-Years'-days are past. I
survive, a jolly candidate for 1821. Another cup of wine
—and while that turncoat bell, that just now mournfully
chanted the obsequies of 1820 departed, with changed
notes lustily rings in a successor, let us attune to its peal
the song made on a like occasion, by hearty, cheerful
Mr. Cotton :

"THE NEW YEAR.

"Hark, the cock crows, and yon bright star
　Tells us, the day himself's not far ;
　And see where, breaking from the night,
　He gilds the western hills with light.
　With him old Janus doth appear,
　Peeping into the future year,
　With such a look as seems to say,
　The prospect is not good that way.
　Thus do we rise ill sights to see,
　And 'gainst ourselves to prophesy ;

When the prophetic fear of things
A more tormenting mischief brings,
More full of soul-tormenting gall
Than direst mischiefs can befall.
But stay! but stay! methinks my sight,
Better informed by clearer light,
Discerns sereneness in that brow,
That all contracted seemed but now.
His reversed face may show distaste,
And frown upon the ills are past;
But that which this way looks is clear,
And smiles upon the New-born Year.
He looks too from a place so high,
The Year lies open to his eye;
And all the moments open are
To the exact discoverer.
Yet more and more he smiles upon
The happy revolution.
Why should we then suspect or fear
The influences of a year?
So smiles upon us the first morn,
And speaks us good so soon as born;
Plague on't! the last was ill enough,
This cannot but make better proof;
Or, at the worst, as we brushed through
The last, why so we may this too;
And then the next in reason should
Be superexcellently good:
For the worst ills (we daily see)
Have no more perpetuity
Than the best fortunes that do fall;
Which also bring us wherewithal
Longer their being to support,
Than those do of the other sort:

And who has one good year in three,
And yet repines at destiny,
Appears ungrateful in the case,
And merits not the good he has.
Then let us welcome the New Guest
With lusty brimmers of the best:
Mirth always should Good Fortune meet,
And renders e'en Disaster sweet:
And though the Princess turn her back,
Let us but line ourselves with sack,
We better shall by far hold out,
Till the next Year she face about."

How say you, reader—do not these verses smack of
the rough magnanimity of the old English vein? Do
they not fortify like a cordial; enlarging the heart, and
productive of sweet blood, and generous spirits, in the
concoction? Where be those puling fears of death, just
now expressed or affected?—Passed like a cloud—absorbed in the purging sunlight of clear poetry—clean
washed away by a wave of genuine Helicon, your only
Spa for these hypochondries.—And now another cup of
the generous! and a merry New Year, and many of
them, to you all, my masters!

MRS. BATTLE'S OPINIONS ON WHIST.

"A CLEAR fire, a clean hearth, and the rigor of the
game." This was the celebrated *wish* of old Sarah Battle
(now with God), who, next to her devotions, loved a
good game of whist. She was none of your lukewarm
gamesters, your half-and-half players, who have no ob-

jection to take a hand, if you want one to make up a
rubber; who affirm that they have no pleasure in winning; that they like to win one game and lose another;
that they can while away an hour very agreeably at a
card-table, but are indifferent whether they play or no;
and will desire an adversary, who has slipped a wrong
card, to take it up and play another. These insufferable
triflers are the curse of a table. One of these flies will
spoil a whole pot. Of such it may be said that they do
not play at cards, but only play at playing at them.

Sarah Battle was none of that breed. She detested
them, as I do, from her heart and soul, and would not,
save upon a striking emergency, willingly seat herself at
the same table with them. She loved a thorough-paced
partner, a determined enemy. She took and gave no
concessions. She hated favors. She never made a re-
voke, nor ever passed it over in her adversary without
exacting the utmost forfeiture. She fought a good fight:
cut and thrust. She held not her good sword (her cards)
"like a dancer." She sat bolt upright, and neither
showed you her cards nor desired to see yours. All
people have their blind side—their superstitions; and I
have heard her declare, under the rose, that hearts was
her favorite suit.

I never in my life—and I knew Sarah Battle many
of the best years of it—saw her take out her snuff-box
when it was her turn to play; or snuff a candle in the
middle of a game; or ring for a servant till it was fairly
over. She never introduced, or connived at, miscellaneous conversation during its process. As she emphati-
cally observed, cards were cards; and if I ever saw un-
mingled distaste in her fine last-century countenance, it
was at the airs of a young gentleman of a literary turn,

who had been with difficulty persuaded to take a hand;
and who, in his excess of candor, declared that he
thought there was no harm in unbending the mind now
and then, after serious studies, in recreations of that
kind! She could not bear to have her noble occupation,
to which she wound up her faculties, considered in that
light. It was her business, her duty, the thing she came
into the world to do—and she did it. She unbent her
mind afterward, over a book.

Pope was her favorite author; his "Rape of the
Lock" her favorite work. She once did me the favor to
play over with me (with the cards) his celebrated game
of ombre in that poem; and to explain to me how far it
agreed with, and in what points it would be found to
differ from, tradrille. Her illustrations were apposite
and poignant; and I had the pleasure of sending the
substance of them to Mr. Bowles; but I suppose they
came too late to be inserted among his ingenious notes
upon that author.

Quadrille, she has often told me, was her first love;
but whist had engaged her maturer esteem. The former, she said, was showy and specious, and likely to
allure young persons. The uncertainty and quick shifting of partners—a thing which the constancy of whist
abhors; the dazzling supremacy and regal investiture of
spadille—absurd, as she justly observed, in the pure aris-
tocracy of whist, where his crown and garter give him
no proper power above his brother nobility of the aces;
the giddy vanity, so taking to the inexperienced, of playing alone; above all, the overpowering attractions of a
Sans Prendre Vole—to the triumph of which there is
certainly nothing parallel or approaching in the contingencies of whist—all these, she would say, make quad-

rille a game of captivation to the young and enthusiastic. But whist was the *solider* game—that was her word. It was a long meal; not, like quadrille, a feast of snatches. One or two rubbers might coextend in duration with an evening. They gave time to form rooted friendships, to cultivate steady enmities. She despised the chance-started, capricious, and ever-fluctuating alliances of the other. The skirmishes of quadrille, she would say, reminded her of the petty, ephemeral embroilments of the little Italian states, depicted by Machiavel: perpetually changing postures and connections; bitter foes to-day, sugared darlings to-morrow; kissing and scratching in a breath; but the wars of whist were comparable to the long, steady, deep-rooted, rational antipathies of the great French and English nations.

A grave simplicity was what she chiefly admired in her favorite game. There was nothing silly in it, like the nob in cribbage—nothing superfluous. No *flushes*—that most irrational of all pleas that a reasonable being can set up!—that any one should claim four by virtue of holding cards of the same mark and color, without reference to the playing of the game, or the individual worth or pretensions of the cards themselves! She held this to be a solecism; as pitiful an ambition at cards as alliteration is in authorship. She despised superficiality, and looked deeper than the colors of things. Suits were soldiers, she would say, and must have a uniformity of ray to distinguish them; but what should we say to a foolish squire, who should claim a merit from dressing up his tenantry in red jackets, that never were to be marshaled—never to take the field? She even wished that whist were more simple than it is; and, in my mind, would have stripped it of some appendages,

which, in the state of human frailty, may be venially,
and even commendably, allowed of. She saw no reason
for the deciding of the trump by the turn of the card.
Why not one suit always trumps? Why two colors,
when the mark of the suits would have sufficiently dis-
tinguished them without it?

"But the eye, my dear madam, is agreeably re-
freshed with the variety. Man is not a creature of
pure reason—he must have his senses delightfully ap-
pealed to. We see it in Roman Catholic countries,
where the music and the paintings draw in many to
worship, whom your Quaker spirit of unsensualizing
would have kept out. You yourself have a pretty collection of paintings—but confess to me, whether walking in your gallery at Sandham, among those clear Van-
dykes, or among the Paul Potters in the anteroom, you
ever felt your bosom glow with an elegant delight, at all
comparable to *that* you have it in your power to experience most evenings over a well-arranged assortment of
the court-cards?—the pretty antic habits, like heralds in
a procession—the gay, triumph-assuring scarlets—the
contrasting, deadly-killing sables—the 'hoary majesty of
spades'—Pam in all his glory!

"All these might be dispensed with; and with their
naked names upon the drab pasteboard, the game might
go on very well, pictureless. But the *beauty* of cards
would be extinguished forever. Stripped of all that is
imaginative in them, they must degenerate into mere
gambling. Imagine a dull, deal board, or drum-head, to
spread them on, instead of that nice verdant carpet (next
to Nature's), fittest arena for those courtly combatants to
play their gallant jousts and tourneys in! Exchange
those delicately-turned ivory markers—(work of Chinese

artist, unconscious of their symbol, or as profanely slighting their true application as the arrantest Ephesian journeyman that turned out those little shrines for the goddess)—exchange them for little bits of leather (our ancestors' money), or chalk and a slate !"

The old lady, with a smile, confessed the soundness of my logic; and to her approbation of my arguments on her favorite topic that evening, I have always fancied myself indebted for the legacy of a curious cribbage-board, made of the finest Sienna marble, which her maternal uncle (old Walter Plumer, whom I have elsewhere celebrated) brought with him from Florence: this, and a trifle of five hundred pounds, came to me at her death.

The former bequest (which I do not least value) I have kept with religious care; though she herself, to confess the truth, was never greatly taken with cribbage. It was an essentially vulgar game, I have heard her say—disputing with her uncle, who was very partial to it. She could never heartily bring her mouth to pronounce " *Go,*" or " *That's a go.*" She called it an ungrammatical game. The pegging teased her. I once knew her to forfeit a rubber (a five-dollar stake), because she would not take advantage of the turn-up knave which would have given it her, but which she must have claimed by the disgraceful tenure of declaring " *two for his heels.*" There is something extremely genteel in this sort of self-denial. Sarah Battle was a gentlewoman born.

Piquet she held the best game at the cards for two persons, though she would ridicule the pedantry of the terms—such as pique—repique—the capot—they savored (she thought) of affectation. But games for two, or even three, she never greatly cared for. She loved the quad-

rate, or square. She would argue thus: Cards are warfare; the ends are gain, with glory. But cards are war,
in disguise of a sport: when single adversaries encounter, the ends proposed are too palpable. By themselves
it is too close a fight; with spectators it is not much bettered. No looker-on can be interested, except for a bet,
and then it is a mere affair of money; he cares not for
your luck *sympathetically*, or for your play.—Three are
still worse; a mere naked war of every man against
every man, as in cribbage, without league or alliance;
or a rotation of petty and contradictory interests, a succession of heartless leagues, and not much more hearty
infractions of them, as in tradrille.—But in square games
(*she meant whist*), all that is possible to be attained in
card-playing is accomplished. There are the incentives
of profit with honor, common to every species—though
the *latter* can be but very imperfectly enjoyed in those
other games, where the spectator is only feebly a partici-
pator. But the parties in whist are spectators and prin-
cipals too. They are a theatre to themselves, and a
looker-on is not wanted. He is rather worse than nothing, and an impertinence. Whist abhors neutrality, or
interests beyond its sphere. You glory in some surpris-
ing stroke of skill or fortune, not because a cold—or
even an interested—by-stander witnesses it, but because
your *partner* sympathizes in the contingency. You win
for two. You triumph for two. Two are exalted. Two
again are mortified; which divides their disgrace, as the
conjunction doubles (by taking off the invidiousness)
your glories. Two losing to two are better reconciled
than one to one in that close butchery. The hostile
feeling is weakened by multiplying the channels. War
becomes a civil game.—By such reasonings as these the

old lady was accustomed to defend her favorite pastime.

No inducement could ever prevail upon her to play at any game, where chance entered into the composition, *for nothing*. Chance, she would argue—and here again admire the subtlety of her conclusion—chance is nothing, but where something else depends upon it. It is obvious that cannot be *glory*. What rational cause of exultation could it give to a man to turn up size ace a hundred times together by himself? or before spectators, where no stake is depending?—Make a lottery of a hundred thousand tickets with but one fortunate number—and what possible principle of our nature, except stupid wonderment, could it gratify to gain that number as many times successively, without a prize? Therefore, she disliked the mixture of chance in backgammon, where it was not played for money. She called it foolish, and those people idiots, who were taken with a lucky hit under such circumstances. Games of pure skill were as little to her fancy. Played for a stake, they were a mere system of overreaching. Played for glory, they were a mere setting of one man's wit—his memory, or combination-faculty rather—against another's; like a mock-engagement at a review, bloodless and profitless. She could not conceive a *game* wanting the spritely infusion of chance, the handsome excuses of good fortune. Two people playing at chess in a corner of a room, while whist was stirring in the centre, would inspire her with insufferable horror and *ennui*. Those well-cut similitudes of Castles, and Knights, the *imagery* of the board, she would argue (and I think in this case justly), were entirely misplaced and senseless. Those hard head-contests can in no instance ally with the fancy. They reject form and color. A pencil and dry slate (she used to say) were the proper arena for such combatants.

To those puny objectors against cards, as nurturing the bad passions, she would retort that man is a gaming animal. He must be always trying to get the better in something or other; that this passion can scarcely be more safely expended than upon a game at cards; that cards are a temporary illusion; in truth, a mere drama; for we do but *play* at being mightily concerned, where a few idle shillings are at stake; yet, during the illusion, we *are* as mightily concerned as those whose stake is crowns and kingdoms. They are a sort of dream-fighting; much ado; great battling, and little bloodshed; mighty means for disproportioned ends; quite as diverting, and a great deal more innoxious, than many of those more serious *games* of life, which men play, without esteeming them to be such.

With great deference to the old lady's judgment in these matters, I think I have experienced some moments in my life, when playing at cards *for nothing* has even been agreeable. When I am in sickness, or not in the best spirits, I sometimes call for the cards, and play a game at piquet *for love* with my cousin Bridget—Bridget Elia.

I grant there is something sneaking in it; but with a toothache, or a sprained ankle—when you are subdued and humble—you are glad to put up with an inferior spring of action.

There is such a thing in nature, I am convinced, as *sick whist*.

I grant it is not the highest style of man—I deprecate the manes of Sarah Battle—she lives not, alas! to whom I should apologize.

At such times, those *terms* which my old friend objected to, come in as something admissible.—I love to get a tierce or a quatorze, though they mean nothing. I am subdued to an inferior interest. Those shadows of winning amuse me.

That last game I had with my sweet cousin (I capotted her)—(dare I tell thee, how foolish I am?)—I wished it might have lasted forever, though we gained nothing, and lost nothing, though it was a mere shade of play: I would be content to go on in that idle folly forever. The pipkin should be ever boiling, that was to prepare the gentle lenitive to my foot, which Bridget was doomed to apply after the game was over: and, as I do not much relish appliances, there it should ever bubble. Bridget and I should be ever playing.

A CHAPTER ON EARS.

I HAVE no ear.—

Mistake me not, reader—nor imagine that I am by nature destitute of those exterior twin appendages, hanging ornaments, and (architecturally speaking) handsome volutes to the human capital. Better my mother had never borne me.—I am, I think, rather delicately than copiously provided with those conduits; and I feel no disposition to envy the mule for his plenty, or the mole for her exactness, in those ingenious labyrinthine inlets —those indispensable side-intelligencers.

Neither have I incurred, or done anything to incur, with Defoe, that hideous disfigurement, which constrained him to draw upon assurance—to feel "quite unabashed," and at ease upon that article. I was never, I thank my stars, in the pillory; nor, if I read them aright, is it within the compass of my destiny that I ever should be.

When, therefore, I say that I have no ear, you will understand me to mean—*for music.* To say that this heart never melted at the concord of sweet sounds, would be a foul self-libel. " *Water parted from the sea* " never fails to move it strangely. So does " *In infancy.*" But they were used to be sung at her harpsichord (the old-fashioned instrument in vogue in those days) by a gentle-woman—the gentlest, sure, that ever merited the appellation—the sweetest—why should I hesitate to name Mrs. S——, once the blooming Fanny Weatheral of the Temple—who had power to thrill the soul of Elia, small imp as he was, even in his long coats, and to make him glow, tremble, and blush with a passion, that not faintly indicated the day-spring of that absorbing sentiment which was afterward destined to overwhelm and subdue his nature quite for Alice W——n.

I even think that *sentimentally* I am disposed to har-mony. But *organically* I am incapable of a tune. I have been practising " *God save the King* " all my life; whistling and humming it over to myself in solitary cor-ners; and am not yet arrived, they tell me, within many quavers of it. Yet hath the loyalty of Elia never been impeached.

I am not without suspicion, that I have an undevel-oped faculty of music within me. For thrumming, in my mild way, on my friend A.'s piano, the other morn-ing, while he was engaged in an adjoining parlor—on his return he was pleased to say, " *he thought it could not be the maid !* " On his first surprise at hearing the keys touched in somewhat an airy and masterful way, not dreaming of me, his suspicions had lighted on *Jenny*. But a grace, snatched from a superior refinement, soon convinced him that some being—technically perhaps deficient, but higher informed from a principle common to all the fine arts—had swayed the keys to a mood which Jenny, with all her (less cultivated) enthusiasm, could never have elicited from them. I mention this as a proof of my friend's penetration, and not with any view of disparaging Jenny.

Scientifically I could never be made to understand (yet have I taken some pains) what a note in music is; or how one note should differ from another. Much less in voices can I distinguish a soprano from a tenor. Only sometimes the thorough-bass I contrive to guess at, from its being supereminently harsh and disagreeable. I tremble, however, for my misapplication of the simplest terms of *that* which I disclaim. While I profess my ignorance, I scarce know what to *say* I am ignorant of. I hate, perhaps, by misnomers. *Sostenuto* and *adagio* stand in the like relation of obscurity to me; and *Sol, Fa, Mi, Re,* is as conjuring as *Baralipton.*

It is hard to stand alone in an age like this—(constituted to the quick and critical perception of all harmonious combinations, I verily believe, beyond all preceding ages, since Jubal stumbled upon the gamut)—to remain, as it were, singly unimpressible to the magic influences of an art which is said to have such an especial stroke at soothing, elevating, and refining the passions.—Yet, rather than break the candid current of my confessions, I must avow to you that I have received a great deal more pain than pleasure from this so cried-up faculty.

I am constitutionally susceptible of noises. A carpenter's hammer, in a warm summer noon, will fret me

into more than midsummer madness. But those uncon-
nected, unset sounds are nothing to the measured malice
of music. The ear is passive to those single strokes;
willingly enduring stripes while it hath no task to con.
To music it cannot be passive. It will strive— mine at
least will—'spite of its inaptitude, to thrid the maze;
like an unskilled eye painfully poring upon hieroglyphics.
I have sat through an Italian Opera, till, for sheer pain,
and inexplicable anguish, I have rushed out into the
noisiest places of the crowded streets, to solace myself
with sounds which I was not obliged to follow, and get
rid of the distracting torment of endless, fruitless, barren
attention! I take refuge in the unpretending assemblage
of honest common-life sounds ; and the purgatory of the
Enraged Musician becomes my paradise.

I have sat at an Oratorio (that profanation of the purposes of the cheerful playhouse) watching the faces of
the auditory in the pit (what a contrast to Hogarth's
Laughing Audience!), immovable, or affecting some
faint emotion, till (as some have said, that our occupations in the next world will be but a shadow of what
delighted us in this) I have imagined myself in some
cold Theatre in Hades, where some of the *forms* of the
earthly one should be kept up, with none of the *enjoyment;* or like that

> —" Party in a parlor
> All silent and all DAMNED."

Above all, these insufferable concertos, and pieces of
music, as they are called, do plague and embitter my apprehension. Words are something ; but to be exposed
to an endless battery of mere sounds; to be long a-dy-
ing, to lie stretched upon a rack of roses; to keep up lan-

guor by unintermitted effort; to pile honey upon sugar, and sugar upon honey, to an interminable, tedious sweetness; to fill up sound with feeling, and strain ideas to keep pace with it; to gaze on empty frames, and be forced to make the pictures for yourself; to read a book, *all stops*, and be obliged to supply the verbal matter; to invent extempore tragedies to answer to the vague gestures of an inexplicable, rambling mime—these are faint shadows of what I have undergone from a series of the ablest-executed pieces of this empty *instrumental music*.

I deny not that, in the opening of a concert, I have experienced something vastly lulling and agreeable; afterward followeth the languor and the oppression. Like that disappointing book in Patmos; or, like the comings on of melancholy, described by Burton, doth Music make her first insinuating approaches: "Most pleasant it is to such as are melancholy given to walk alone in some solitary grove, betwixt wood and water, by some brook-side, and to meditate upon some delightsome and pleasant subject, which shall affect him most, *amabilis insania*, and *mentis gratissimus error*. A most incomparable delight to build castles in the air, to go smiling to themselves, acting an infinite variety of parts, which they suppose, and strongly imagine, they act, or that they see done. So delightsome these toys at first, they could spend whole days and nights without sleep, even whole years in such contemplations and fantastical meditations, which are like so many dreams, and will hardly be drawn from them—winding and unwinding themselves as so many clocks, and still pleasing their humors until at last the SCENE TURNS UPON A SUDDEN, and they being now habitated to such meditations and solitary places, can endure no company, can think of nothing but harsh and distasteful subjects. Fear, sorrow, suspicion, *subrusticus pudor*, discontent, cares, and weariness of life, surprise them on a sudden, and they can think of nothing else; continually suspecting, no sooner are their eyes open, but this infernal plague of melancholy seizeth on them and terrifies their souls, representing some dismal object to their minds; which now, by no means, no labor, no persuasions, they can avoid, they cannot be rid of, they cannot resist."

Something like this "scene turning" I have experienced at the evening-parties at the house of my good Catholic friend *Nov——*, who, by the aid of a capital organ, himself the most finished of players, converts his drawing-room into a chapel, his week-days into Sundays, and these latter into minor heaven.*

When my friend commences upon one of those solemn anthems, which peradventure struck upon my heedless ear, rambling in the side aisles of the dim Abbey, some five-and-thirty years since, waking a new sense, and putting a soul of old religion into my young apprehension—(whether it be *that*, in which the Psalmist, weary of the persecutions of bad men, wisheth to himself dove's wings; or *that other*, which, with a like measure of sobriety and pathos, inquireth by what means the young man shall best cleanse his mind)—a holy calm pervadeth me. I am for the time

> —" rapt above earth,
> And possess joys not promised at my birth."

But when this master of the spell, not content to have laid a soul prostrate, goes on, in his power, to in-

---

* " I have been there, and still would go;
  'Tis like a little heaven below."—Dr. Watts.

flict more bliss than lies in her capacity to receive, impatient to overcome her " earthly " with his "heavenly " —still pouring in, for protracted hours, fresh waves and fresh from the sea of sound, or from that inexhausted *German* ocean, above which, in triumphant progress, dolphin-seated, ride those Arions *Haydn* and *Mozart*, with their attendant Tritons, *Bach*, *Beethoven*, and a countless tribe, whom to attempt to reckon up would but plunge me again in the deeps—I stagger under the weight of harmony, reeling to and fro at my wits' end; clouds, as of frankincense, oppress me—priests, altars, censers, dazzle before me—the genius of *his* religion hath me in her toils—a shadowy triple tiara invests the brow of my friend, late so naked, so ingenuous—he is Pope, and by him sits, like as in the anomaly of dreams, a she-Pope, too, tri-coroneted like himself!—I am converted, and yet a Protestant; at once *malleus hereticorum*, and myself grand heresiarch: or three heresies centre in my person: I am Marcion, Ebion, and Cerinthus—Gog and Magog—what not?—till the coming in of the friendly supper-tray dissipates the figment, and a draught of true Lutheran beer (in which chiefly my friend shows himself no bigot) at once reconciles me to the rationalities of a purer faith, and restores to me the genuine, unterrifying aspects of my pleasant - countenanced host and hostess.

ALL-FOOLS'-DAY.

THE compliments of the season to my worthy masters, and a merry first of April to us all!

Many happy returns of this day to you—and you—

and *you*, Sir—nay, never frown, man, nor put a long face upon the matter. Do not we know one another? what need of ceremony among friends? we have all a touch of *that same*—you understand me—a speck of the motley. Beshrew the man who on such a day as this, the *general festival*, should affect to stand aloof. I am none of those sneakers. I am free of the corporation, and care not who knows it. He that meets me in the forest to-day, shall meet with no wiseacre, I can tell him. *Stultus sum.* Translate me that, and take the meaning of it to yourself for your pains. What! man, we have four quarters of the globe on our side, at the least computation.

Fill us a cup of that sparkling gooseberry—we will drink no wise, melancholy, politic port on this day—and let us troll the catch of Amiens—*duc ad me—duc ad me* —how goes it?—

> " Here shall he see
> Gross fools as he."

Now would I give a trifle to know historically and authentically who was the greatest fool that ever lived. I would certainly give him a bumper. Marry, of the present breed, I think I could without much difficulty name you the party.

Remove your cap a little farther, if you please: it hides my bauble. And now each man bestride his hobby, and dust away his bells to what tune he pleases. I will give you, for my part,

> —" The crazy old church-clock,
> And the bewildered chimes."

Good Master Empedocles, you are welcome. It is long since you went a salamander-gathering down Etna. Worse than samphire-picking by some odds. 'Tis a mercy your worship did not singe your mustachios.

Ha! Cleombrotus! and what salads in faith did you light upon at the bottom of the Mediterranean? You were founder, I take it, of the disinterested sect of the Calenturists.

Gebir, my old freemason, and prince of plasterers at Babel, bring in your trowel, most Ancient Grand! You have claim to a seat here at my right hand, as patron of the stammerers. You left your work, if I remember Herodotus correctly, at eight hundred million toises, or thereabout, above the level of the sea. Bless us, what a long bell you must have pulled, to call your top workmen to their nuncheon on the low grounds of Shinar! Or, did you send up your garlic and onions by a rocket? I am a rogue if I am not ashamed to show you our Monument on Fish Street Hill, after your altitudes. Yet we think it somewhat.

What, the magnanimous Alexander in tears?—cry baby, put its finger in its eye, it shall have another globe, round as an orange, pretty moppet!

Mister Adams——'odso, I honor your coat—pray do us the favor to read to us that sermon, which you lent to Mistress Slipslop—the twenty-and-second in your portmanteau there—on Female Incontinence—the same—it will come in most irrelevantly and impertinently seasonable to the time of the day. •

Good Master Raymund Lully, you look wise. Pray correct that error.—

Duns, spare your definitions. I must fine you a bumper, or a paradox. We will have nothing said or done syllogistically this day. Remove those logical forms, waiter, that no gentleman break the tender shins of his apprehension stumbling across them.

Master Stephen, you are late.—Ha! Cokes, is it you?

—Aguecheek, my dear knight, let me pay my devoir to you.—Master Shallow, your worship's poor servant to command.—Master Silence, I will use few words with you.—Slender, it shall go hard if I edge not you in somewhere.—You six will engross all the poor wit of the company to-day.—I know it, I know it.

Ha! honest R——, my fine old Librarian of Ludgate, time out of mind, art thou here again?   Bless my doublet, it is not over-new; threadbare as thy stories—what dost thou flitting about the world at this rate?—Thy customers are extinct, defunct, bed-rid, have ceased to read long ago.—Thou goest still among them, seeing if, peradventure, thou canst hawk a volume or two.—Good Granville S——, thy last patron, is flown.

> "King Pandion, he is dead,
>   All thy friends are lapt in lead."—

Nevertheless, noble R——, come in, and take your seat here, between Armado and Quisada; for in true courtesy, in gravity, in fantastic smiling to thyself, in courteous smiling upon others, in the goodly ornature of well-appareled speech, and the commendation of wise sentences, thou art nothing inferior to those accomplished Dons of Spain.   The spirit of chivalry forsake me forever, when I forget thy singing the song of Macheath, which declares that he might be *happy with either*, situated between those two ancient spinsters—when I forget the inimitable formal love which thou didst make, turning now to the one, and now to the other, with that Malvolian smile—as if Cervantes, not Gay, had written it for his hero; and as if thousands of periods must revolve, before the mirror of courtesy could have given his invidious preference between a pair of so goodly-propertied and meritorious-equal damsels. . . .

To descend from these altitudes, and not to protract our Fools' Banquet beyond its appropriate day—for I fear the Second of April is not many hours distant—in sober verity I will confess a truth to thee, reader. I love a *Fool*—as naturally, as if I were of kith and kin to him. When a child, with childlike apprehensions, that dived not below the surface of the matter, I read those *Parables*—not guessing at the involved wisdom—I had more yearnings toward that simple architect, that built his house upon the sand, than I entertained for his more cautious neighbor: I grudged at the hard censure pronounced upon the quiet soul that kept his talent; and—prizing their simplicity beyond the more provident, and, to my apprehension, somewhat *unfeminine* wariness of their competitors—I felt a kindliness, that almost amounted to a *tendre*, for those five thoughtless virgins.—I have never made an acquaintance since, that lasted: or a friendship, that answered; with any that had not some tincture of the absurd in their characters. I venerate an honest obliquity of understanding. The more laughable blunders a man shall commit in your company, the more tests he giveth you, that he will not betray or overreach you. I love the safety, which a palpable hallucination warrants; the security, which a word out of season ratifies. And take my word for this, reader, and say a fool told it you, if you please, that he who hath not a dram of folly in his mixture, hath pounds of much worse matter in his composition. It is observed, that "the foolisher the fowl or fish—woodcocks—dotterels—cods'-heads, etc.—the finer the flesh thereof," and what are commonly the world's received fools, but such whereof the world is not worthy? and what have been some of the kindliest patterns of our species, but so many darlings

of absurdity, minions of the goddess, and her white boys?
—Reader, if you wrest my words beyond their fair con-
struction, it is you and not I, that are the *April Fool*.

A QUAKERS' MEETING.

" Still-born Silence! thou that art
  Flood-gate of the deeper heart!
  Offspring of a heavenly kind!
  Frost o' the mouth, and thaw o' the mind!
  Secrecy's confidant, and He
  Who makes religion mystery!
  Admiration's speaking'st tongue!
  Leave, thy desert shades among,
  Reverend hermits' hallowed cells,
  Where retired Devotion dwells!
  With thy enthusiasms come,
  Seize our tongues, and strike us dumb."*

READER, wouldst thou know what true peace and
quiet mean; wouldst thou find a refuge from the noises
and clamors of the multitude; wouldst thou enjoy at
once solitude and society; wouldst thou possess the
depth of thine own spirit in stillness, without being shut
out from the consolatory faces of thy species; wouldst
thou be alone, and yet accompanied; solitary, yet not
desolate; singular, yet not without some to keep thee
in countenance; a unit in aggregate; a simple in com-
posite: come with me into a Quakers' meeting.

Dost thou love silence deep as that " before the winds
were made?" go not out into the wilderness; descend

* From " Poems of all Sorts," by Richard Fleckno, 1653.

not into the profundities of the earth; shut not up thy
casements, nor pour wax into the little cells of thy ears,
with little-faithed, self-mistrusting Ulysses.—Retire with
me into a Quakers' meeting.

For a man to refrain even from good words, and to
hold his peace, it is commendable; but for a multitude,
it is great mastery.

What is the stillness of the desert compared with
this place? what the uncommunicating muteness of
fishes?—here the goddess reigns and revels.—" Boreas,
and Cesias, and Argestes loud," do not with their inter-
confounding uproars more augment the brawl—nor the
waves of the blown Baltic with their clubbed sounds—
than their opposite (Silence her sacred self) is multiplied
and rendered more intense by numbers, and by sympathy. She, too, hath her deeps that call unto deeps. Negation itself hath a positive more and less; and closed eyes
would seem to obscure the great obscurity of midnight.

There are wounds which an imperfect solitude cannot
heal. By imperfect I mean that which a man enjoyeth
by himself. The perfect is that which he can sometimes
attain in crowds, but nowhere so absolutely as in a
Quakers' meeting.—Those first hermits did certainly understand this principle when they retired into Egyptian
solitudes, not singly, but in shoals, to enjoy one another's
want of conversation. The Carthusian is bound to his
brethren by this agreeing spirit of incommunicative-
ness. In secular occasions, what so pleasant as to be
reading a book through a long, winter evening, with a
friend sitting by—say a wife—he, or she, too (if that be
probable), reading another, without interruption or oral
communicaton?—can there be no sympathy without the
gabble of words?—away with this inhuman, shy, single,

shade-and-cavern-haunting solitariness. Give me, Master
Zimmermann, a sympathetic solitude.

To pace along in the cloisters or side-aisles of some
cathedral, time-stricken—

> " Or under hanging mountains,
>   Or by the fall of fountains "— `

is but a vulgar luxury, compared with that which those
enjoy who come together for the purposes of more complete, abstracted solitude.   This is the loneliness " to be
felt."—The Abbey church of Westminster hath nothing
so solemn, so spirit-soothing, as the naked walls and
benches of a Quakers' meeting.   Here are no tombs, no
inscriptions,

> —" Sands, ignoble things,
>   Dropped from the ruined sides of kings "—

but here is something which throws Antiquity herself
into the foreground — SILENCE — eldest of things—language of old Night—primitive Discourser—to which the
insolent decays of mouldering grandeur have but arrived
by a violent, and, as we may say, unnatural progression.

> " How reverend is the view of these hushed heads,
>   Looking tranquillity ! "

Nothing - plotting, naught - caballing, unmischievous
synod! convocation without intrigue! parliament without debate! what a lesson dost thou read to council, and
to consistory!—if my pen treat of you lightly—as haply
it will wander—yet my spirit hath gravely felt the wisdom of your custom, when sitting among you in deepest
peace, which some out-welling tears would rather confirm
than disturb, I have reverted to the times of your begin-
nings, and the sowings of the seed by Fox and Dewesbury.

I have witnessed that which brought before my eyes your heroic tranquillity, inflexible to the rude jests and serious violences of the insolent soldiery, republican or royalist, sent to molest you—for ye sate betwixt the fires of two persecutions, the outcast and offscouring of church and presbytery.—I have seen the reeling sea-ruffian, who had wandered into your receptacle with the avowed intention of disturbing your quiet, from the very spirit of the place receive in a moment a new heart, and presently sit among ye as a lamb among lambs. And I remember Penn before his accusers, and Fox in the bail-dock, where he was lifted up in spirit, as he tells us, and "the judge and the jury became as dead men under his feet."

Reader, if you are not acquainted with it, I would recommend to you, above all church-narratives, to read Sewel's History of the Quakers. It is in folio, and is the abstract of the Journals of Fox and the primitive Friends. It is far more edifying and affecting than anything you will read of Wesley and his colleagues. Here is nothing to stagger you, nothing to make you mistrust, no suspicion of alloy, no drop or dreg of the worldly or ambitious spirit. You will here read the true story of that much-injured, ridiculed man (who, perhaps, hath been a by-word in your mouth)—James Naylor: what dreadful sufferings, with what patience, he endured, even to the boring through of his tongue with red-hot irons, without a murmur; and with what strength of mind, when the delusion he had fallen into, which they stigmatized for blasphemy, had given way to clearer thoughts, he could renounce his error, in a strain of the beautifullest humility, yet keep his first grounds, and be a Quaker still!—so different from the practice of your common converts from enthusiasm, who, when they apostatize, *apostatize all*, and think they can never get far enough from the society of their former errors, even to the renunciation of some saving truths, with which they had been mingled, not implicated.

Get the Writings of John Woolman by heart; and love the early Quakers.

How far the followers of these good men in our days have kept to the primitive spirit, or in what proportion they have substituted formality for it, the Judge of Spirits can alone determine. I have seen faces in their assemblies, upon which the dove sate visibly brooding. Others again I have watched, when my thoughts should have been better engaged, in which I could possibly detect nothing but a blank inanity. But quiet was in all, and the disposition to unanimity, and the absence of the fierce controversial workings. If the spiritual pretensions of the Quakers have abated, at least they make few pretenses. Hypocrites they certainly are not, in their preaching. It is seldom, indeed, that you shall see one get up among them to hold forth. Only now and then a trembling female, generally *ancient*, voice is heard—you cannot guess from what part of the meeting it proceeds —with a low, buzzing, musical sound, laying out a few words which "she thought might suit the condition of some present," with a quaking diffidence, which leaves no possibility of supposing that anything of female vanity was mixed up, where the tones were so full of tenderness, and a restraining modesty. The men, for what I have observed, speak seldomer.

Once only, and it was some years ago, I witnessed a sample of the old Foxian orgasm. It was a man of giant stature, who, as Wordsworth phrases it, might have danced "from head to foot equipt in iron mail." His

frame was of iron, too. But *he* was malleable. I saw
him shake all over with the spirit—I dare not say of delusion. The strivings of the outer man were unutterra-
ble—he seemed not to speak, but to be spoken from. I
saw the strong man bowed down, and his knees to fail—
his joints all seemed loosening—it was a figure to set off
against Paul Preaching—the words he uttered were few,
and sound—he was evidently resisting his will—keeping
down his own word-wisdom with more mighty effort,
than the world's orators strain for theirs. "He had been
a wit in his youth," he told us, with expressions of a sober remorse. And it was not till long after the impression had begun to wear away, that I was enabled, with
something like a smile, to recall the striking incongruity
of the confession—understanding the term in its worldly
acceptation—with the frame and physiognomy of the
person before me. His brow would have scared away
the Levities—the Jocos Risus-que—faster than the Loves
fled the face of Dis at Enna. By *wit*, even in his youth,
I will be sworn he understood something far within the
limits of an allowable liberty.

More frequently the meeting is broken up without a
word having been spoken. But the mind has been fed.
You go away with a sermon not made with hands. You
have been in the milder caverns of Trophonius; or as in
some den, where that fiercest and savagest of all wild
creatures, the Tongue, that unruly member, has strangely lain tied up and captive. You have bathed with stillness. Oh, when the spirit is sore fretted, even tired to
sickness of the janglings, the nonsense-noises of the
world, what a balm and a solace it is, to go and seat
yourself, for a quiet half-hour, upon some undisputed
corner of a bench, among the gentle Quakers!

Their garb and stillness conjoined, present a uniformity, tranquil and herd-like—as in the pasture—"forty feeding like one."—

The very garments of a Quaker seem incapable of receiving a soil; and cleanliness in them to be something more than the absence of its contrary. Every Quakeress is a lily; and when they come up in bands to their Whitsun-conferences, whitening the easterly streets of the metropolis, from all parts of the United Kingdom, they show like troops of the Shining Ones.

THE OLD AND THE NEW SCHOOLMASTER.

MY reading has been lamentably desultory and immethodical. Odd, out-of-the-way, old English plays, and treatises, have supplied me with most of my notions, and ways of feeling. In everything that relates to *science*, I am a whole Encyclopædia behind the rest of the world. I should have scarcely cut a figure among the franklins, or country gentlemen, in King John's days. I know less geography than a schoolboy of six weeks' standing. To me a map of old Ortelius is as authentic as Arrowsmith. I do not know whereabout Africa merges into Asia; whether Ethiopia lie in one or other of those great divisions; nor can form the remotest conjecture of the position of New South Wales, or Van Diemen's Land. Yet do I hold a correspondence with a very dear friend in the first-named of these two Terræ Incognitæ. I have no astronomy. I do not know where to look for the Bear, or Charles's Wain; the place of any star; or the name of any of them at sight. I guess at Venus only by

her brightness—and if the sun on some portentous morn
were to make his first appearance in the West, I verily
believe, that, while all the world were gasping in apprehension about me, I alone should stand unterrified, from
sheer incuriosity and want of observation. Of history
and chronology I possess some vague points, such as one
cannot help picking up in the course of miscellaneous
study; but I never deliberately sat down to a chronicle,
even of my own country. I have most dim apprehensions of the four great monarchies; and sometimes the
Assyrian, sometimes the Persian, floats as *first*, in my
fancy. I make the widest conjectures concerning Egypt,
and her shepherd kings. My friend *M.*, with great pains-
taking, got me to think I understood the first proposition
in Euclid, but gave me over in despair at the second. I
am entirely unacquainted with the modern languages;
and, like a better man than myself, have "small Latin
and less Greek." I am a stranger to the shapes and
texture of the commonest trees, herbs, flowers—not from
the circumstance of my being town-born—for I should
have brought the same inobservant spirit into the world
with me, had I first seen it " on Devon's leafy shores "—
and am no less at a loss among purely town-objects,
tools, engines, mechanic processes. Not that I affect
ignorance—but my head has not many mansions, nor
spacious; and I have been obliged to fill it with such
cabinet curiosities as it can hold without aching. I
sometimes wonder how I have passed my probation
with so little discredit in the world, as I have done, upon
so meagre a stock. But the fact is, a man may do very
well with a very little knowledge, and scarce be found
out, in mixed company; everybody is so much more
ready to produce his own, than to call for a display of

6

your acquisitions. But in a *tête-à-tête* there is no shuffling. The truth will out. There is nothing which I dread so much as the being left alone for a quarter of an hour with a sensible, well-informed man, that does not know me. I lately got into a dilemma of this sort.

In one of my daily jaunts between Bishopsgate and Shacklewell, the coach stopped to take up a staid-looking gentleman, about the wrong side of thirty, who was giving his parting directions (while the steps were adjusting), in a tone of mild authority, to a tall youth, who seemed to be neither his clerk, his son, nor his servant, but something partaking of all three. The youth was dismissed, and we drove on. As we were the sole passengers, he naturally enough addressed his conversation to me; and we discussed the merits of the fare, the civility and punctuality of the driver; the circumstance of an opposition coach having been lately set up, with the probabilities of its success—to all which I was enabled to return pretty satisfactory answers, having been drilled into this kind of etiquette by some years' daily practice of riding to and fro in the stage aforesaid—when he suddenly alarmed me by a startling question, whether I had seen the show of prize cattle that morning in Smithfield? Now, as I had not seen it, and do not greatly care for such sort of exhibitions, I was obliged to return a cold negative. He seemed a little mortified, as well as astonished, at my declaration, as (it appeared) he was just come fresh from the sight, and doubtless had hoped to compare notes on the subject. However, he assured me that I had lost a fine treat, as it far exceeded the show of last year. We were now approaching Norton Folgate, when the sight of some shop-goods *ticketed* freshened him up into a dissertation upon the cheapness of cottons this spring. I was now a little in heart, as the nature of my morning avocations had brought me into some sort of familiarity with the raw material; and I was surprised to find how eloquent I was becoming on the state of the India market—when, presently, he dashed my incipient vanity to the earth at once, by inquiring whether I had ever made any calculation as to the value of the rental of all the retail shops in London. Had he asked of me, what song the Siren sang, or what name Achilles assumed when he hid himself among women, I might, with Sir Thomas Browne, have hazarded a "wide solution." * My companion saw my embarrassment, and, the alms-houses beyond Shoreditch just coming in view, with great good-nature and dexterity, shifted his conversation to the subject of public charities; which led to the comparative merits of provision for the poor in past and present times, with observations on the old monastic institutions, and charitable orders; but, finding me rather dimly impressed with some glimmering notions from old poetic associations, than strongly fortified with any speculations reducible to calculation on the subject, he gave the matter up; and, the country beginning to open more and more upon us, as we approached the turnpike at Kingsland (the destined termination of his journey), he put a home-thrust upon me, in the most unfortunate position he could have chosen, by advancing some queries relative to the North-Pole Expedition. While I was muttering out something about the panorama of those strange regions (which I had actually seen), by way of parrying the question, the coach stopping relieved me from any further apprehensions. My companion getting out, left me in the comfortable possession

* Urn Burial.

of my ignorance; and I heard him, as he went off, putting questions to an outside passenger, who had alighted with him, regarding an epidemic disorder, that had been rife about Dalston, and which my friend assured him had gone through five or six schools in that neighborhood. The truth now flashed upon me, that my companion was a schoolmaster; and that the youth, whom he had parted from at our first acquaintance, must have been one of the bigger boys, or the usher. He was evidently a kind-hearted man, who did not seem so much desirous of provoking discussion by the questions which he put, as of obtaining information at any rate. It did not appear that he took any interest, either, in such kind of inquiries, for their own sake; but that he was in some way bound to seek for knowledge. A greenish-colored coat, which he had on, forbade me to surmise that he was a clergyman. The adventure gave birth to some reflections on the difference between persons of his profession in past and present times.

Rest to the souls of those fine old pedagogues; the breed, long since extinct, of the Lilys and the Linacres: who, believing that all learning was contained in the languages which they taught, and despising every other acquirement as superficial and useless, came to their task as to a sport! Passing from infancy to age, they dreamed away all their days as in a grammar-school. Revolving in a perpetual cycle of declensions, conjugations, syntaxes, and prosodies; renewing constantly the occupations which had charmed their studious childhood; rehearsing continually the part of the past; life must have slipped from them at last like one day. They were always in their first garden, reaping harvests of their golden time, among their *Flori* and their *Spici-*

legia; in Arcadia still, but kings! the ferule of their sway not much harsher, but of like dignity with that mild sceptre attributed to King Basileus; the Greek and Latin, their stately Pamela and their Philoclea; with the occasional duncery of some untoward tyro, serving for a refreshing interlude of a Mopsa or a clown Damœtas!

With what a savor doth the Preface to Colet's, or (as it is sometimes called) Paul's Accidence, set forth! "To exhort every man to the learning of grammar, that intendeth to attain the understanding of the tongues, wherein is contained a great treasury of wisdom and knowledge, it would seem but vain and lost labor; for so much as it is known, that nothing can surely be ended whose beginning is either feeble or faulty; and no building be perfect whereas the foundation and groundwork is ready to fall, and unable to hold the burden of the frame." How well doth this stately preamble (comparable to those which Milton commendeth as "having been the usage to prefix to some solemn law, then first promulgated by Solon or Lycurgus") correspond with and illustrate that pious zeal for conformity, expressed in a succeeding clause, which would fence about grammar-rules with the severity of faith articles!—"as for the diversity of grammars, it is well profitably taken away by the Kings Majesties wisdom, who foreseeing the inconvenience, and favourably providing the remedie, caused one kind of grammar by sundry learned men to be diligently drawn, and so to be set out, only everywhere to be taught, for the use of learners, and·for the hurt in changing of schoolmaisters." What a *gusto* in that which follows: "wherein it is profitable that he [the pupil] can orderly decline his noun, and his verb." *His* noun!

The fine dream is fading away fast; and the least

concern of a teacher in the present day is to inculcate grammar-rules.

The modern schoolmaster is expected to know a little of everything, because his pupil is required not to be entirely ignorant of anything. He must be superficially, if I may so say, omniscient. He is to know something of pneumatics; of chemistry; of whatever is curious, or proper to excite the attention of the youthful mind; an insight into mechanics is desirable, with a touch of statistics; the quality of soils, etc., botany, the constitution of his country, *cum multis aliis*. You may get a notion of some part of his expected duties by consulting the famous Tractate on Education addressed to Mr. Hartlib.

All these things—these, or the desire of them—he is expected to instill, not by set lessons from professors, which he may charge in the bill, but at school intervals, as he walks the streets, or saunters through green fields (those natural instructors), with his pupils. The least part of what is expected from him, is to be done in school-hours. He must insinuate knowledge at the *mollia tempora fandi*. He must seize every occasion— the season of the year; the time of the day; a passing cloud; a rainbow; a wagon of hay; a regiment of soldiers going by—to inculcate something useful. He can receive no pleasure from a casual glimpse of Nature, but must catch at it as an object of instruction. He must interpret beauty into the picturesque. He cannot relish a beggar-man, or a gypsy, for thinking of the suitable improvement. Nothing comes to him, not spoiled by the sophisticating medium of moral uses. The Universe —that Great Book, as it has been called—is to him indeed, to all intents and purposes, a book out of which he is doomed to read tedious homilies to distasting

schoolboys. Vacations themselves are none to him, he
is only rather worse off than before; for commonly he
has some intrusive upper boy fastened upon him at such
times; some cadet of a great family; some neglected
lump of nobility, or gentry; that he must drag after him
to the play, to the Panorama, to Mr. Bartley's Orrery,
to the Panopticon, or into the country, to a friend's
house, or his favorite watering-place. Wherever he
goes, this uneasy shadow attends him. A boy is at his
board, and in his path, and in all his movements. He is
boy-rid, sick of perpetual boy.

Boys are capital fellows in their own way, among
their mates; but they are unwholesome companions for
grown people. The restraint is felt no less on the one
side than on the other. Even a child, that "plaything
for an hour," tires *always*. The noises of children,
playing their own fancies—as I now hearken to them
by fits, sporting on the green before my window, while
I am engaged in these grave speculations at my neat
suburban retreat at Shacklewell—by distance made more
sweet—inexpressibly take from the labor of my task.
It is like writing to music. They seem to modulate my
periods. They ought at least to do so—for in the voice
of that tender age there is a kind of poetry, far unlike
the harsh prose accents of man's conversation. I should
but spoil their sport, and diminish my own sympathy
for them, by mingling in their pastime.

I would not be domesticated all my days with a person of very superior capacity to my own—not, if I know
myself at all, from any considerations of jealousy or self-
comparison, for the occasional communion with such
minds has constituted the fortune and felicity of my life
—but the habit of too constant intercourse with spirits

above you, instead of raising you, keeps you down.
Too frequent doses of original thinking from others re-
strain what lesser portion of that faculty you may possess of your own. You get entangled in another man's
mind, even as you lose yourself in another man's grounds.
You are walking with a tall varlet, whose strides out-
pace yours to lassitude. The constant operation of such
potent agency would reduce me, I am convinced, to im-
becility. You may derive thoughts from others; your
way of thinking, the mould in which your thoughts are
cast, must be your own. Intellect may be imparted, but
not each man's intellectual frame.—

As little as I should wish to be always thus dragged
upward, as little (or, rather, still less) is it desirable to
be stunted downward by your associates. The trumpet
does not more stun you by its loudness than a whisper
teases you by its provoking inaudibility.

Why are we never quite at our ease in the presence
of a schoolmaster? Because we are conscious that he is
not quite at his ease in ours. He is awkward and out of
place in the society of his equals. He comes like Gulli-
ver from among his little people, and he cannot fit the
stature of his understanding to yours. He cannot meet
you on the square. He wants a point given him, like an
indifferent whist-player. He is so used to teaching that
he wants to be teaching *you*. One of these professors,
upon my complaining that these little sketches of mine
were anything but methodical, and that I was unable to
make them otherwise, kindly offered to instruct me in
the method by which young gentlemen in *his* seminary
were taught to compose English themes.—The jests of a
schoolmaster are coarse or thin. They do not *tell* out
of school. He is under the restraint of a formal or di-

dactive hypocrisy in company, as a clergyman is under a
moral one. He can no more let his intellect loose in society than the other can his inclinations. He is forlorn
among his coevals; his juniors cannot be his friends.

"I take blame to myself," said a sensible man of this
profession, writing to a friend respecting a youth who
had quitted his school abruptly, "that your nephew was
not more attached to me. But persons in my situation
are more to be pitied than can well be imagined. We
are surrounded by young and, consequently, ardently
affectionate hearts, but *we* can never hope to share an
atom of their affections. The relation of master and
scholar forbids this. '*How pleasing this must be to you,
how I envy your feelings!*' my friends will sometimes say
to me, when they see young men whom I have educated
return, after some years' absence from school, their eyes
shining with pleasure while they shake hands with their
old master, bringing a present of game to me or a toy to
my wife, and thanking me in the warmest terms for my
care of their education. A holiday is begged for the
boys; the house is a scene of happiness; I, only, am
sad at heart. — This fine-spirited and warm-hearted
youth, who fancies he repays his master with gratitude
for the care of his boyish years—this young man, in the
eight long years I watched over him with a parent's anxiety, never could repay me with one look of genuine
feeling. He was proud when I praised; he was submis-
sive when I reproved him; but he did never *love* me;
and what he now mistakes for gratitude and kindness
for me is but the pleasant sensation which all persons
feel at revisiting the scenes of their boyish hopes and
fears; and the seeing on equal terms the man they were
accustomed to look up to with reverence. My wife,

too," this interesting correspondent goes on to say, "my once darling Anna, is the wife of a schoolmaster.—When I married her—knowing that the wife of a schoolmaster ought to be a busy, notable creature, and fearing that my gentle Anna would ill supply the loss of my dear, bustling mother, just then dead, who never sat still, was in every part of the house in a moment, and whom I was obliged sometimes to threaten to fasten down in a chair to save her from fatiguing herself to death—I expressed my fears that I was bringing her into a way of life unsuitable to her; and she, who loved me tenderly, promised for my sake to exert herself to perform the duties of her new situation. She promised, and she has kept her word. What wonders will not woman's love perform? My house is managed with a propriety and decorum unknown in other schools; my boys are well fed, look healthy, and have every proper accommodation; and all this performed with a careful economy that never descends to meanness. But I have lost my gentle, *helpless* Anna! When we sit down to enjoy an hour of repose after the fatigue of the day, I am compelled to listen to what have been her useful (and they are really useful) employments through the day, and what she proposes for her to-morrow's task. Her heart and her features are changed by the duties of her situation. To the boys, she never appears other than the *master's wife*, and she looks up to me as the *boy's master*, to whom all show of love and affection would be highly improper, and unbecoming the dignity of her situation and mine. Yet *this* my gratitude forbids me to hint to her. For my sake she submitted to be this altered creature, and can I reproach her for it?"—For the communication of this letter, I am indebted to my cousin Bridget.

VALENTINE'S-DAY.

HAIL to thy returning festival, old Bishop Valentine! Great is thy name in the rubric, thou venerable arch-flamen of Hymen! Immortal go-between! who and what manner of person art thou? Art thou but a *name*, typifying the restless principle which impels poor humans to seek perfection in union? or wert thou, indeed, a mortal prelate, with thy tippet and thy rochet, thy apron on, and decent lawn sleeves? Mysterious personage! like unto thee, assuredly, there is no other mitred father in the calendar; not Jerome, nor Ambrose, nor Cyril, nor the consigner of undipped infants to eternal torments, Austin, whom all mothers hate; nor he who hated all mothers, Origen; nor Bishop Bull, nor Archbishop Parker, nor Whitgift. Thou comest attended with thousands and ten thousands of little loves, and the air is

"Brushed with the hiss of rustling wings."

Singing Cupids are thy choristers and thy precentors; and instead of the crosier, the mystical arrow is borne before thee.

In other words, this is the day on which those charming little missives, ycleped Valentines, cross and inter-cross each other at every street and turning. The weary and all forspent twopenny-postman sinks beneath a load of delicate embarrassments not his own. It is scarcely credible to what an extent this ephemeral courtship is carried on in this loving town, to the great enrichment of porters, and detriment of knockers and bell-wires. In these little visual interpretations, no emblem is so common as the *heart*—that little, three-cornered exponent of our hopes and fears—the bestuck and bleeding heart. It is twisted and tortured into more allegories and affectations than an opera-hat. What authority we have in history or mythology for placing the headquarters and metropolis of God Cupid in this anatomical seat rather than in any other, is not very clear; but we have got it, and it will serve as well as any other. Else we might easily imagine—upon some other system which might have prevailed for anything which our pathology knows to the contrary—a lover addressing his mistress, in perfect simplicity of feeling, "Madam, my *liver* and fortune are entirely at your disposal;" or putting a delicate question, "Amanda, have you a *midriff* to bestow?" But custom has settled these things, and awarded the seat of sentiment to the aforesaid triangle, while its less fortunate neighbors wait at animal and anatomical distance.

Not many sounds in life, and I include all urban and all rural sounds, exceed in interest a *knock at the door.* It "gives a very echo to the throne where Hope is seated." But its issues seldom answer to this oracle within. It is so seldom that just the person we want to see comes. But of all the clamorous visitations the welcomest in expectation is the sound that ushers in, or seems to usher in, a Valentine. As the raven himself was hoarse that announced the fatal entrance of Duncan, so the knock of the postman on this day is light, airy, confident, and befitting one that bringeth good tidings. It is less mechanical than on other days. You will say, "That is not the post I am sure." Visions of Love, of Cupids, of Hymens! —delightful eternal commonplaces, which, "having been, will always be;" which no schoolboy nor schoolman can write away; having your irreversible throne in the fancy and affections—what are your transports, when the happy maiden, opening with careful finger, careful not to break the emblematic seal, bursts upon the sight of some well-designed allegory, some type, some youthful fancy, not without verses—

> "Lovers all,
> A madrigal,"

or some such device, not over abundant in sense—young Love disclaims it—and not quite silly—something between wind and water, a chorus where the sheep might almost join the shepherd, as they did, or as I apprehend they did, in Arcadia.

All Valentines are not foolish; and I shall not easily forget thine, my kind friend—if I may have leave to call you so—E. B. E. B. lived opposite a young maiden, whom he had often seen, unseen, from his parlor-window in C—e Street. She was all joyousness and innocence, and just of an age to enjoy receiving a Valentine, and just of a temper to bear the disappointment of missing one with good-humor. E. B. is an artist of no common powers—in the fancy parts of designing, perhaps, inferior to none. His name is known at the bottom of many a well-executed vignette in the way of his profession, but no further—for E. B. is modest, and the world meets nobody half-way. E. B. meditated how he could repay this young maiden for many a favor which she had done him unknown; for when a kindly face greets us, though but passing by, and never knows us again, nor we it, we should feel it as an obligation; and E. B. did. This good artist set himself at work to please the damsel. It was just before Valentine's-day three years since. He wrought, unseen and unsuspected, a wondrous work.

We need not say it was on the finest gilt paper with borders—full, not of common hearts and heartless allegory, but all the prettiest stories of love from Ovid, and older poets than Ovid (for E. B. is a scholar). There was Pyramus and Thisbe, and be sure Dido was not forgot, nor Hero and Leander, and swans more than sang in Cayster, with mottoes and fanciful devices, such as beseemed—a work in short of magic. Iris dipped the woof. This on Valentine's-eve he commended to the all-swallowing, indiscriminate orifice—O ignoble trust!—of the common post; but the humble medium did its duty, and from his watchful stand the next morning he saw the cheerful messenger knock, and by-and-by the precious charge delivered. He saw, unseen, the happy girl unfold the Valentine, dance about, clap her hands, as one after one the pretty emblems unfolded themselves. She danced about, not with light love, or foolish expectations, for she had no lover; or, if she had, none she knew that could have created those bright images which delighted her. It was more like some fairy present; a God-send, as our familiarly pious ancestors termed a benefit received where the benefactor was unknown. It would do her no harm. It would do her good forever after. It is good to love the unknown. I only give this as a specimen of E. B. and his modest way of doing a concealed kindness.

Good-morrow to my Valentine, sings poor Ophelia; and no better wish, but with better auspices, we wish to all faithful lovers, who are not too wise to despise old legends, but are content to rank themselves humble diocesans of old Bishop Valentine and his true church.

IMPERFECT SYMPATHIES.

I am of a constitution so general, that it consorts and sympathizeth with all things; I have no antipathy, or rather idiosyncrasy in anything. Those natural repugnancies do not touch me, nor do I behold with prejudice the French, Italian, Spaniard, or Dutch.—*Religio Medici.*

THAT the author of the Religio Medici, mounted upon the airy stilts of abstraction, conversant about notional and conjectural essences; in whose categories of Being the possible took the upper hand of the actual; should have overlooked the impertinent individualities of such poor concretions as mankind, is not much to be admired. It is rather to be wondered at, that in the genus of animals he should have condescended to distinguish that species at all. For myself—earth-bound and fettered to the scene of my activities—

"Standing on earth, not rapt above the sky,"

I confess that I do feel the differences of mankind, national or individual, to an unhealthy excess. I can look with no indifferent eye upon things or persons. Whatever is, is to me a matter of taste or distaste; or when once it becomes indifferent, it begins to be disrelishing. I am, in plainer words, a bundle of prejudices—made up of likings and dislikings—the veriest thrall to sympathies, apathies, antipathies. In a certain sense, I hope it may be said of me that I am a lover of my species. I can feel for all indifferently, but I cannot feel toward all equally. The more purely-English word that expresses sympathy, will better explain my meaning. I can be a friend to a worthy man, who upon another account cannot be my mate or *fellow*. I cannot *like* all people alike.*

I have been trying all my life to like Scotchmen, and am obliged to desist from the experiment in despair. They cannot like me—and in truth, I never knew one of that nation who attempted to do it. There is something more plain and ingenuous in their mode of proceeding. We know one another at first sight. There is an order of imperfect intellects (under which mine must be content to rank) which in its constitution is essentially anti-Caledonian. The owners of the sort of faculties I allude to, have minds rather suggestive than comprehensive. They have no pretenses to much clearness or precision

* I would be understood as confining myself to the subject of *imperfect sympathies*. To nations or classes of men there can be no direct antipathy. There may be individuals born and constellated so opposite to another individual nature that the same sphere cannot hold them. I have met with my moral antipodes, and can believe the story of two persons meeting (who never saw one another before in their lives) and instantly fighting.

> "—We by proof find there should be
> 'Twixt man and man such an antipathy,
> That though he can show no just reason why
> For any former wrong or injury,
> Can neither find a blemish in his fame,
> Nor aught in face or feature justly blame,
> Can challenge or accuse him of no evil,
> Yet, notwithstanding, hates him as a devil."

The lines are from old Heywood's "Hierarchie of Angels," and he subjoins a curious story in confirmation, of a Spaniard who attempted to assassinate a King Ferdinand of Spain, and being put to the rack could give no other reason for the deed but an inveterate antipathy which he had taken to the first sight of the King.

> "—The cause which to that act compelled him
> Was, he ne'er loved him since he first beheld him."

in their ideas, or in their manner of expressing them.
Their intellectual wardrobe (to confess fairly) has few
whole pieces in it.   They are content with fragments
and scattered pieces of Truth.   She presents no full front
to them—a feature or side-face at the most.   Hints and
glimpses, germs and crude essays at a system, is the utmost they pretend to.   They beat up a little game peradventure—and leave it to knottier heads, more robust
constitutions, to run it down.   The light that lights them
is not steady and polar, but mutable and shifting: waxing, and again waning.   Their conversation is accordingly.   They will throw out a random word in or out of
season, and be content to let it pass for what it is worth.
They cannot speak always as if they were upon their oath
—but must be understood, speaking or writing, with some
abatement.   They seldom wait to mature a proposition,
but e'en bring it to market in the green ear.   They delight to impart their defective discoveries as they arise,
without waiting for their development.   They are no
systematizers, and would but err more by attempting it.
Their minds, as I said before, are suggestive merely.   The
brain of a true Caledonian (if I am not mistaken) is constituted upon quite a different plan.   His Minerva is born
in panoply.   You are never admitted to see his ideas in
their growth—if, indeed, they do grow, and are not rather
put together upon principles of clock-work.   You never
catch his mind in an undress.   He never hints or suggests
anything, but unlades his stock of ideas in perfect order
and completeness.   He brings his total wealth into company, and gravely unpacks it.   His riches are always
about him.   He never stoops to catch a glittering something in your presence to share it with you, before he
quite knows whether it be true touch or not.   You can-

7

not cry *halves* to anything that he finds. He does not
find, but brings. You never witness his first apprehension of a thing. His understanding is always at its meridian—you never see the first dawn, the early streaks.
—He has no falterings of self-suspicion. Surmises,
guesses, misgivings, half-intuitions, semi-consciousnesses,
partial illuminations, dim instincts, embryo conceptions,
have no place in his brain, or vocabulary. The twilight
of dubiety never falls upon him. Is he orthodox—he has
no doubts. Is he an infidel—he has none either. Between the affirmative and the negative there is no border-
land with him. You cannot hover with him upon the
confines of truth, or wander in the maze of a probable
argument. He always keeps the path. You cannot
make excursions with him—for he sets you right. His
taste never fluctuates. His morality never abates. He
cannot compromise, or understand middle actions. There
can be but a right and a wrong. His conversation is as
a book. His affirmations have the sanctity of an oath.
You must speak upon the square with him. He stops a
metaphor like a suspected person in an enemy's country.
"A healthy book!"—said one of his countrymen to me,
who had ventured to give that appellation to John Buncle.—"Did I catch rightly what you said? I have heard
of a man in health, and of a healthy state of body, but I
do not see how that epithet can be properly applied to a
book." Above all, you must beware of indirect expressions before a Caledonian. Clap an extinguisher upon
your irony, if you are unhappily blest with a vein of it.
Remember you are upon your oath. I have a print of
a graceful female after Leonardo da Vinci, which I was
showing off to Mr. ——. After he had examined it minutely, I ventured to ask him how he liked MY BEAUTY

(a foolish name it goes by among my friends)—when he very gravely assured me that "he had considerable respect for my character and talents" (so he was pleased to say), "but had not given himself much thought about the degree of my personal pretensions." The misconception staggered me, but did not seem much to disconcert him. Persons of this nation are particularly fond of affirming a truth—which nobody doubts. They do not so properly affirm, as annunciate it. They do, indeed, appear to have such a love of truth (as if, like virtue, it were valuable for itself) that all truth becomes equally valuable, whether the proposition that contains it be new or old, disputed, or such as is impossible to become a subject of disputation. I was present not long since at a party of North Britons, where a son of Burns was expected; and happened to drop a silly expression (in my South British way), that I wished it were the father instead of the son—when four of them started up at once to inform me that "that was impossible, because he was dead." An impracticable wish, it seems, was more than they could conceive. Swift has hit off this part of their character, namely, their love of truth, in his biting way, but with an illiberality that necessarily confines the passage to the margin.* The tedious-

* There are some people who think they sufficiently acquit themselves, and entertain their company, with relating facts of no consequence, not at all out of the road of such common incidents as happen every day; and this I have observed more frequently among the Scots than any other nation, who are very careful not to omit the minutest circumstances of time or place; which kind of discourse, if it were not a little relieved by the uncouth terms and phrases, as well as accent and gesture peculiar to that country, would be hardly tolerable.—*Hints toward an Essay on Conversation.*

ness of these people is certainly provoking. I wonder
if they ever tire one another? In my early life I had a
passionate fondness for the poetry of Burns. I have
sometimes foolishly hoped to ingratiate myself with his
countrymen by expressing it. But I have always found
that a true Scot resents your admiration of his compat-
riot, even more than he would your contempt of him.
The latter he imputes to your "imperfect acquaintance
with many of the words which he uses;" and the same
objection makes it a presumption in you to suppose that
you can admire him. Thomson they seem to have forgotten. Smollett they have neither forgotten nor forgiven, for his delineation of Rory and his companion,
upon their first introduction to our metropolis. Speak
of Smollett as a great genius, and they will retort upon
you Hume's History compared with *his* Continuation of it.
What if the historian had continued Humphrey Clinker?

I have, in the abstract, no disrespect for Jews. They
are a piece of stubborn antiquity, compared with which
Stonehenge is in its nonage. They date beyond the pyra-
mids. But I should not care to be in habits of familiar
intercourse with any of that nation. I confess that I
have not the nerves to enter their synagogues. Old
prejudices cling about me. I cannot shake off the story
of Hugh of Lincoln. Centuries of injury, contempt, and
hate, on the one side—of cloaked revenge, dissimulation,
and hate, on the other, between our and their fathers,
must and ought to affect the blood of the children. I
cannot believe it can run clear and kindly yet; or that a
few fine words, such as candor, liberality, the light of a
nineteenth century, can close up the breaches of so dead-
ly a disunion. A Hebrew is nowhere congenial to me.
He is least distasteful on 'Change—for the mercantile

spirit levels all distinctions, as all are beauties in the
dark. I boldly confess that I do not relish the approxi-
mation of Jew and Christian, which has become so fashionable. The reciprocal endearments have, to me, something hypocritical and unnatural in them. I do not like
to see the Church and Synagogue kissing and congeeing
in awkward postures of an affected civility. If *they* are
converted, why do they not come over to us altogether?
Why keep up a form of separation when the life of it is
fled? If they can sit with us at table, why do they keck
at our cookery? I do not understand these half convert-
ites. Jews Christianizing—Christians Judaizing—puzzle
me. I like fish or flesh. A moderate Jew is a more
confounding piece of anomaly than a wet Quaker. The
spirit of the synagogue is essentially *separative*. B——
would have been more in keeping if he had abided by
the faith of his forefathers. There is a fine scorn in his
face, which Nature meant to be of —— Christians. The
Hebrew spirit is strong in him, in spite of his prosely-
tism. He cannot conquer the Shibboleth. How it breaks
out when he sings, "The Children of Israel passed through
the Red Sea!" The auditors, for the moment, are as
Egyptians to him, and he rides over our necks in triumph. There is no mistaking him. B—— has a strong
expression of sense in his countenance, and it is confirmed
by his singing. The foundation of his vocal excellence
is sense. He sings with understanding, as Kemble delivered dialogue. He would sing the Commandments,
and give an appropriate character to each prohibition.
His nation, in general, have not over-sensible counte-
nances. How should they?—but you seldom see a silly
expression among them. Gain, and the pursuit of gain,
sharpen a man's visage. I never heard of an idiot be-

ing born among them. Some admire the Jewish female physiognomy. I admire it—but with trembling. Jael had those full, dark, inscrutable eyes.

In the negro countenance you will often meet with strong traits of benignity. I have felt yearnings of tenderness toward some of these faces—or rather masks—that have looked out kindly upon one in casual encounters in the streets and highways. I love what Fuller beautifully calls—these "images of God out in ebony." But I should not like to associate with them, to share my meals and my good nights with them—because they are black.

I love Quaker ways and Quaker worship. I venerate the Quaker principles. It does me good for the rest of the day when I meet any of their people in my path. When I am ruffled or disturbed by any occurrence, the sight, or quiet voice of a Quaker, acts upon me as a ventilator, lightening the air, and taking off a load from the bosom. But I cannot like the Quakers (as Desdemona would say) "to live with them." I am all over sophisticated—with humors, fancies, craving hourly sympathy. I must have books, pictures, theatres, chit-chat, scandal, jokes, ambiguities, and a thousand whimwhams, which their simpler taste can do without. I should starve at their primitive banquet. My appetites are too high for the salads which (according to Evelyn) Eve dressed for the angel, my gusto too excited

"To sit a guest with Daniel at his pulse."

The indirect answers which Quakers are often found to return to a question put to them, may be explained, I think, without the vulgar assumption that they are more given to evasion and equivocating than other peo-

ple. They naturally look to their words more carefully,
and are more cautious of committing themselves. They
have a peculiar character to keep up on this head. They
stand in a manner upon their veracity. A Quaker is by
law exempted from taking an oath. The custom of
resorting to an oath in extreme cases, sanctified as it is
by all religious antiquity, is apt (it must be confessed)
to introduce into the laxer sort of minds the notion of
two kinds of truth—the one applicable to the solemn
affairs of justice, and the other to the common proceedings of daily intercourse. As truth bound upon the conscience by an oath can be but truth, so in the common
affirmations of the shop and the market-place a latitude
is expected, and conceded upon questions wanting this
solemn covenant. Something less than truth satisfies.
It is common to hear a person say, "You do not expect
me to speak as if I were upon my oath." Hence a great
deal of incorrectness and inadvertency, short of falsehood, creeps into ordinary conversation; and a kind of
secondary or laic-truth is tolerated, where clergy-truth—
oath-truth, by the nature of the circumstances, is not
required. A Quaker knows none of this distinction.
His simple affirmation being received, upon the most
sacred occasions, without any further test, stamps a
value upon the words which he is to use upon the most
indifferent topics of life. He looks to them, naturally,
with more severity. You can have of him no more
than his word. He knows, if he is caught tripping in a
casual expression, he forfeits, for himself at least, his
claim to the invidious exemption. He knows that his
syllables are weighed—and how far a consciousness of
this particular watchfulness, exerted against a person,
has a tendency to produce indirect answers, and a di-

verting of the question by honest means, might be il-
lustrated, and the practice justified, by a more sacred
example than is proper to be adduced upon this occasion.   The admirable presence of mind, which is notorious in Quakers upon all contingencies, might be traced
to this imposed self-watchfulness—if it did not seem
rather an humble and secular scion of that old stock of
religious constancy, which never bent or faltered, in the
Primitive Friends, or gave way to the winds of persecution, to the violence of judge or accuser, under trials and
racking examinations.   " You will never be the wiser, if
I sit here answering your questions till midnight," said
one of those upright Justicers to Penn, who had been
putting law-cases with a puzzling subtlety.   "Thereafter
as the answers may be," retorted the Quaker.   The as-
tonishing composure of this people is sometimes ludi-
crously displayed in lighter instances.   I was traveling
in a stage-coach with three male Quakers, buttoned up
in the straitest nonconformity of their sect.   We stopped
to bait at Andover, where a meal, partly tea-apparatus,
partly supper, was set before us.   My friends confined
themselves to the tea-table.   I in my way took supper.
When the landlady brought in the bill, the eldest of my
companions discovered that she had charged for both
meals.   This was resisted.   Mine hostess was very clamorous and positive.   Some mild arguments were used on
the part of the Quakers, for which the heated mind of
the good lady seemed by no means a fit recipient.   The
guard came in with his usual peremptory notice.   The
Quakers pulled out their money and formally tendered
it—so much for tea—I, in humble imitation, tendering
mine—for the supper which I had taken.   She would not
relax in her demand. So they all three quietly put up their

silver, as did myself, and marched out of the room, the
eldest and gravest going first, with myself closing up the
rear, who thought I could not do better than follow the
example of such grave and warrantable personages. We
got in. The steps went up. The coach drove off. The
murmurs of mine hostess, not very indistinctly or ambig-
uously pronounced, became after a time inaudible—and
now my conscience, which the whimsical scene had for
a while suspended, beginning to give some twitches, I
waited, in the hope that some justification would be
offered by these serious persons for the seeming injustice
of their conduct. To my great surprise not a syllable
was dropped on the subject. They sat as mute as at a
meeting. At length the eldest of them broke silence,
by inquiring of his next neighbor, "Hast thee heard
how indigos go at the India House?" and the question
operated as a soporific on my moral feeling as far as
Exeter.

WITCHES, AND OTHER NIGHT-FEARS.

We are too hasty when we set down our ancestors in
the gross for fools, for the monstrous inconsistencies (as
they seem to us) involved in their creed of witchcraft.
In the relations of this visible world we find them to
have been as rational, and shrewd to detect an historic
anomaly, as ourselves. But when once the invisible
world was supposed to be opened, and the lawless agency of bad spirits assumed, what measures of probability,
of decency, of fitness, or proportion—of that which dis-
tinguishes the likely from the palpable absurd—could
they have to guide them in the rejection or admission of

any particular testimony? That maidens pined away, wasting inwardly as their waxen images consumed before a fire—that corn was lodged, and cattle lamed—that whirlwinds uptore in diabolic revelry the oaks of the forest— or that spits and kettles only danced a fearful-innocent vagary about some rustic's kitchen when no wind was stirring—were all equally probable where no law of agency was understood.   That the prince of the powers of darkness, passing by the flower and pomp of the earth, should lay preposterous siege to the weak fantasy of indigent eld, has neither likelihood nor unlikehood *a priori* to us, who have no measure to guess at his policy, or standard to estimate what rate those anile souls may fetch in the devil's market.   Nor, when the wicked are expressly symbolized by a goat, was it to be wondered at so much that *he* should come sometimes in that body, and assert his metaphor.   That the intercourse was opened at all between both worlds was, perhaps, a mistake; but that once assumed, I see no reason for disbelieving one attested story of this nature more than another on the score of absurdity.   There is no law to judge of the lawless, or canon by which a dream may be criticised.

I have sometimes thought that I could not have existed in the days of received witchcraft; that I could not have slept in a village where one of those reputed hags dwelt. Our ancestors were bolder or more obtuse. Amid the universal belief that these wretches were in league with the author of all evil, holding hell tributary to their muttering, no simple justice of the peace seems to have scrupled issuing, or silly head-borough serving, a warrant upon them—as if they should subpœna Satan! Prospero in his boat, with his books and wand about him, suffers

himself to be conveyed away at the mercy of his enemies to an unknown island. He might have raised a
storm or two, we think, on the passage. His acquies-
cence is in exact analogy to the non-resistance of witches
to the constituted powers. What stops the fiend in
Spenser from tearing Guyon to pieces—or who had
made it a condition of his prey, that Guyon must take
assay of the glorious bait?—we have no guess. We do
not know the laws of that country.

From my childhood I was extremely inquisitive about
witches and witch-stories. My maid, and more legendary aunt, supplied me with good store. But I shall mention the accident which directed my curiosity originally
into this channel. In my father's book-closet, the "History of the Bible," by Stackhouse, occupied a distin-
guished station. The pictures with which it abounds—
one of the ark, in particular, and another of Solomon's
temple, delineated with all the fidelity of ocular admeas-
urement, as if the artist had been upon the spot—attract-
ed my childish attention. There was a picture, too, of
the Witch raising up Samuel, which I wish that I had
never seen. We shall come to that hereafter. Stackhouse is in two huge tomes—and there was a pleasure in
removing folios of that magnitude, which, with infinite
straining, was as much as I could manage, from the situation which they occupied upon an upper shelf. I have not
met with the work from that time to this, but I remember
it consisted of Old Testament stories, orderly set down,
with the *objection* appended to each story, and the *solution*
of the objection regularly tacked to that. The *objection*
was a summary of whatever difficulties had been opposed
to the probability of the history, by the shrewdness of
ancient or modern infidelity, drawn up with an almost

complimentary excess of candor. The *solution* was brief, modest, and satisfactory. The bane and antidote were both before you. To doubts so put, and so quashed, there seemed to be an end forever. The dragon lay dead, for the foot of the veriest babe to trample on. But—like as was rather feared than realized from that slain monster in Spenser—from the womb of those crushed errors young dragonets would creep, exceeding the prowess of so tender a Saint George as myself to vanquish. The habit of expecting objections to every passage, set me upon starting more objections, for the glory of finding a solution of my own for them. I became staggered and perplexed, a skeptic in long-coats. The pretty Bible-stories which I had read, or heard read in church, lost their purity and sincerity of impression, and were turned into so many historic or chronologic theses to be defended against whatever impugners. I was not to disbelieve them, but—the next thing to that—I was to be quite sure that some one or other would or had disbelieved them. Next to making a child an infidel, is the letting him know that there are infidels at all. Credulity is the man's weakness, but the child's strength. Oh, how ugly sound scriptural doubts from the mouth of a babe and a suckling! I should have lost myself in these mazes, and have pined away, I think, with such unfit sustenance as these husks afforded, but for a fortunate piece of ill-fortune, which about this time befell me. Turning over the picture of the ark with too much haste, I unhappily made a breach in its ingenious fabric; driving my inconsiderate fingers right through the two larger quadrupeds —the elephant and the camel—that stare (as well they might) out of the last two windows next the steerage in that unique piece of naval architecture. Stackhouse was henceforth looked up, and became an interdicted treasure. With the book, the *objections* and *solutions* gradually cleared out of my head, and have seldom returned since in any force to trouble me. But there was one impression which I had imbibed with Stackhouse, which no lock or bar could shut out, and which was destined to try my childish nerves rather more seriously.—That detestable picture.

I was dreadfully alive to nervous terrors. The night-time, solitude, and the dark, were my hell. The sufferings I endured in this nature would justify the expression. I never laid my head on my pillow, I suppose, from the fourth to the seventh or eighth year of my life—so far as memory serves in things so long ago—without an assurance, which realized its own prophecy, of seeing some frightful spectre. Be old Stackhouse then acquitted in part, if I say that to his picture of the witch raising up Samuel—(O that old man covered with a mantle!)—I owe, not my midnight terrors, the hell of my infancy, but the shape and manner of their visitation. It was he who dressed up for me a hag that nightly sate upon my pillow—a sure bedfellow, when my aunt or my maid was far from me. All day long, while the book was permitted me, I dreamed waking over his delineation, and at night (if I may use so bold an expression) awoke into sleep, and found the vision true. I durst not, even in the daylight, once enter the chamber where I slept, without my face turned to the window, aversely from the bed where my witch-ridden pillow was. Parents do not know what they do when they leave tender babes alone to go to sleep in the dark. The feeling about for a friendly arm—the hoping for a familiar voice, when they awake screaming, and find none to soothe them, what a terrible shaking it is to their poor nerves! The keeping them up till midnight, through candle-light and the unwholesome hours, as they are called, would, I am satisfied, in a medical point of view, prove the better caution. That detestable picture, as I have said, gave the fashion to my dreams, if dreams they were, for the scene of them was invariably the room in which I lay. Had I never met with the picture, the fears would have come self-pictured in some shape or other—

"Headless bear, black man, or ape"—

but, as it was, my imaginations took that form. It is not book, or picture, or the stories of foolish servants, which create these terrors in children. They can at most but give them a direction. Dear little T. H., who of all children has been brought up with the most scrupulous exclusion of every taint of superstition, who was never allowed to hear of goblin or apparition, or scarcely to be told of bad men, or to read or hear of any distressing story, finds all this world of fear, from which he has been so rigidly excluded *ab extra*, in his own "thick-coming fancies;" and from his little midnight pillow, this nurse-child of optimism will start at shapes, unborrowed of tradition, in sweats to which the reveries of the cell-damned murderer are tranquillity.

Gorgons, and Hydras, and Chimæras dire—stories of Celæno and the Harpies—may reproduce themselves in the brain of superstition—but they were there before. They are transcripts, types—the archetypes are in us, and eternal. How else should the recital of that, which we know in a waking sense to be false, come to affect us at all? or

—"Names, whose sense we see not,
Fray us with things that be not?"

Is it that we naturally conceive terror from such objects, considered in their capacity of being able to inflict upon us bodily injury? Oh, least of all! These terrors are of older standing. They date beyond body, or, without the body, they would have been the same. All the cruel, tormenting, defined devils in Dante, tearing, mangling, choking, stifling, scorching demons—are they one-half so fearful to the spirit of a man, as the simple idea of a spirit unembodied following him—

> " Like one that on a lonesome road
> Doth walk in fear and dread,
> And having once turned round, walks on
> And turns no more his head ;
> Because he knows a frightful fiend
> Doth close behind him tread." *

That the kind of fear here treated of is purely spiritual—that it is strong in proportion as it is objectless upon earth—that it predominates in the period of sinless infancy—are difficulties, the solution of which might afford some probable insight into our antemundane condition, and a peep at least into the shadow-land of preëxistence.

My night-fancies have long ceased to be afflictive. I confess an occasional nightmare; but I do not, as in early youth, keep a stud of them. Fiendish faces, with the extinguished taper, will come and look at me; but I know them for mockeries, even while I cannot elude their presence, and I fight and grapple with them. For the credit of my imagination, I am almost ashamed to say how tame and prosaic my dreams are grown. They are never romantic, seldom even rural. They are of architecture and of buildings—cities abroad, which I have

* Mr. Coleridge's Ancient Mariner.

never seen and hardly have hoped to see. I have traversed, for the seeming length of a natural day, Rome,
Amsterdam, Paris, Lisbon—their churches, palaces,
squares, market-places, shops, suburbs, ruins, with an
inexpressible sense of delight—a map-like distinctness
of trace—and a daylight vividness of vision, that was all
but being awake. I have formerly traveled among the
Westmoreland fells—my highest Alps—but they are objects too mighty for the grasp of my dreaming recognition; and I have again and again awoke with ineffectual
struggles of the inner eye, to make out a shape, in any
way whatever, of Helvellyn. Methought I was in that
country, but the mountains were gone. The poverty of
my dreams mortifies me. There is Coleridge, at his will
can conjure up icy domes, and pleasure-houses for Kubla
Khan, and Abyssinian maids, and songs of Abara, and
caverns—

" Where Alph, the sacred river, runs "—

to solace his night solitudes—when I cannot muster a
fiddle. Barry Cornwall has his tritons and his nereids
gamboling before him in nocturnal visions, and proclaim-
ing sons born to Neptune—when my stretch of imaginative activity can hardly, in the night-season, raise up the
ghost of a fish-wife. To set my failures in somewhat a
mortifying light—it was after reading the noble Dream
of this poet, that my fancy ran strong upon these marine
spectra; and the poor plastic power, such as it is, within
me set to work, to humor my folly in a sort of dream
that very night. Methought I was upon the ocean-bil-
lows at some sea-nuptials, riding and mounted high, with
the customary train sounding their conchs before me (I
myself, you may be sure, the *leading god*), and jollily we

went careering over the main, till just where Ino Leuco-
thea should have greeted me (I think it was Ino) with a
white embrace, the billows gradually subsiding, fell from
a sea-roughness to a sea-calm, and thence to a river-mo-
tion, and that river (as happens in the familiarization of
dreams) was no other than the gentle Thames, which
landed me in the wafture of a placid wave or two, alone,
safe and inglorious, somewhere at the foot of Lambeth
Palace.

The degree of the soul's creativeness in sleep might
furnish no whimsical criterion of the quantum of poetical faculty resident in the same soul waking. An old
gentleman, a friend of mine, and a humorist, used to
carry this notion so far that, when he saw any stripling
of his acquaintance ambitious of becoming a poet, his
first question would be, "Young man, what sort of
dreams have you?" I have so much faith in my old
friend's theory that, when I feel that idle vein returning
upon me, I presently subside into my proper element of
prose, remembering those eluding nereids, and that in-
auspicious inland landing.

MY RELATIONS.

I AM arrived at that point of life at which a man may
account it a blessing, as it is a singularity, if he have
either of his parents surviving. I have not that felicity
—and sometimes think feelingly of a passage in Browne's
Christian Morals, where he speaks of a man that hath
lived sixty or seventy years in the world. "In such a
compass of time," he says, "a man may have a close ap-

prehension what it is to be forgotten, when he hath lived
to find none who could remember his father, or scarcely
the friends of his youth, and may sensibly see with what
a face in no long time OBLIVION will look upon himself."

I had an aunt, a dear and good one. She was one
whom single blessedness had soured to the world. She
often used to say that I was the only thing in it which
she loved; and, when she thought I was quitting it, she
grieved over me with mother's tears. A partiality quite
so exclusive my reason cannot altogether approve. She
was from morning till night poring over good books, and
devotional exercises. Her favorite volumes were Thomas
à Kempis, in Stanhope's translation; and a Roman Catholic Prayer Book, with the *matins* and *complines* regularly set down—terms which I was that time too young to
understand. She persisted in reading them, although
admonished daily concerning their Papistical tendency;
and went to church every Sabbath as a good Protestant
should do. These were the only books she studied;
though I think, at one period of her life, she told me, she
had read with great satisfaction the Adventures of an
Unfortunate Young Nobleman. Finding the door of the
chapel in Essex Street open one day—it was in the infancy of that heresy—she went in, liked the sermon, and the
manner of worship, and frequented it at intervals for
some time after. She came not for doctrinal points, and
never missed them. With some little asperities in her
constitution, which I have above hinted at, she was a
steadfast, friendly being, and a fine *old Christian.* She
was a woman of strong sense, and a shrewd mind—extraordinary at a *repartie;* one of the few occasions of
her breaking silence—else she did not much value wit.
The only secular employment I remember to have seen

her engaged in, was, the splitting of French beans, and dropping them into a china basin of fair water. The odor of those tender vegetables to this day comes back upon my senses, redolent of soothing recollections. Certainly it is the most delicate of culinary operations.

Male aunts, as somebody calls them, I had none—to remember. By the uncle's side I may be said to have been born an orphan. Brother, or sister, I never had any—to know them. A sister, I think, that should have been Elizabeth, died in both our infancies. What a comfort, or what a care, may I not have missed in her?—But I have cousins sprinkled about in Hertfordshire—besides *two*, with whom I have been all my life in habits of the closest intimacy, and whom I may term cousins *par excellence*. These are James and Bridget Elia. They are older than myself by twelve, and ten, years; and neither of them seems disposed, in matters of advice and guidance, to waive any of the prerogatives which primogeniture confers. May they continue still in the same mind; and when they shall be seventy-five, and seventy-three, years old (I cannot spare them sooner), persist in treating me in my grand climacteric precisely as a stripling or younger brother!

James is an inexplicable cousin. Nature hath her unities, which not every critic can penetrate; or, if we feel, we cannot explain them. The pen of Yorick, and of none since his, could have drawn J. E. entire—those fine Shandean lights and shades, which make up his story. I must limp after in my poor antithetical manner, as the fates have given me grace and talent. J. E. then—to the eye of a common observer at least—seemeth made up of contradictory principles. The genuine child of impulse, the frigid philosopher of prudence—the phlegm of my cousin's doctrine is invariably at war with his temperament, which is high sanguine. With always some fire-new project in his brain, J. E. is the systematic opponent of innovation, and crier down of everything that has not stood the test of age and experiment. With a hundred fine notions chasing one another hourly in his fancy, he is startled at the least approach to the romantic in others; and, determined by his own sense in everything, commends *you* to the guidance of common-sense on all occasions.—With a touch of the eccentric in all which he does, or says, he is only anxious that *you* should not commit yourself by doing anything absurd or singular. On my once letting slip at the table, that I was not fond of a certain popular dish, he begged me at any rate not to *say* so—for the world would think me mad. He disguises a passionate fondness for works of high art (whereof he hath amassed a choice collection), under the pretext of buying only to sell again—that his enthusiasm may give no encouragement to yours. Yet, if it were so, why does that piece of tender, pastoral Domenichino hang still by his wall?—is the ball of his sight much more dear to him?—or what picture-dealer can talk like him?

Whereas mankind, in general, are observed to warp their speculative conclusions to the bent of their individual humors, *his* theories are sure to be in diametrical opposition to his constitution. He is courageous as Charles of Sweden, upon instinct; chary of his person upon principle, as a traveling Quaker.—He has been preaching up to me, all my life, the doctrine of bowing to the great—the necessity of forms, and manner, to a man's getting on in the world. He himself never aims at either, that I can discover—and has a spirit that would stand upright in the presence of the Cham of Tartary. It is pleasant to

hear him discourse of patience—extolling it as the truest
wisdom—and to see him during the last seven minutes
that his dinner is getting ready. Nature never ran up in
her haste a more restless piece of workmanship than
when she moulded this impetuous cousin—and Art never
turned out a more elaborate orator than he can display
himself to be, upon this favorite topic of the advantages
of quiet and contentedness in the state, whatever it be,
that we are placed in. He is triumphant on this theme,
when he has you safe in one of those short stages that
ply for the western road, in a very obstructing manner,
at the foot of John Murray's Street—where you get in
when it is empty, and are expected to wait till the vehi-
cle hath completed her just freight—a trying three-quarters of an hour to some people. He wonders at your
fidgetiness—" where could we be better than we are, *thus
sitting, thus consulting?* "—" prefers, for his part, a state
of rest to locomotion"—with an eye all the while upon
the coachman—till at length, waxing out of all patience,
at *your want of it,* he breaks out into a pathetic remonstrance at the fellow for detaining us so long over the
time which he had professed, and declares peremptorily,
that "the gentleman in the coach is determined to get
out, if he does not drive on that instant."

Very quick at inventing an argument, or detecting a
sophistry, he is incapable of attending *you* in any chain
of arguing. Indeed, he makes wild work with logic: and
seems to jump at most admirable conclusions by some process, not at all akin to it. Consonantly enough to this,
he hath been heard to deny, upon certain occasions, that
there exists such a faculty at all in man as *reason;* and
wondereth how man came first to have a conceit of it—
enforcing his negation with all the might of *reasoning* he

is master of. He has some speculative notions against laughter, and will maintain that laughing is not natural to *him*—when peradventure the next moment his lungs shall crow like Chanticleer. He says some of the best things in the world—and declareth that wit is his aversion. It was he who said, upon seeing the Eton boys at play in their grounds—*What a pity to think that these fine ingenuous lads in a few years will all be changed into frivolous Members of Parliament!*

His youth was fiery, glowing, tempestuous—and in age he discovereth no symptom of cooling. This is that which I admire in him. I hate people who meet Time half-way. I am for no compromise with that inevitable spoiler. While he lives, J. E. will take his swing. It does me good, as I walk toward the street of my daily avocation, on some fine May morning, to meet him marching in a quite opposite direction, with a jolly, handsome presence, and shining, sanguine face, that indicates some purchase in his eye—a Claude—or a Hobbima—for much of his enviable leisure is consumed at Christie's and Phillips's—or where not, to pick up pictures, and such gauds. On these occasions he mostly stopped me, to read a short lecture on the advantage a person like me possesses above himself, in having his time occupied with business which he *must* do—assureth me that he often feels it hang heavy on his hands—wishes he had fewer holidays—and goes off—Westward Ho!—chanting a tune, to Pall Mall—perfectly convinced that he has convinced me—while I proceed in my opposite direction tuneless.

It is pleasant again to see this Professor of Indifference doing the honors of his new purchase, when he has fairly housed it. You must view it in every light, till *he* has found the best—placing it at this distance, and at that, but always suiting the focus of your sight to his own. You must spy at it through your fingers, to catch the aërial perspective—though you assure him that to you the landscape shows much more agreeable without that artifice. Woe be to the luckless wight, who does not only not respond to his rapture, but who should drop an unseasonable intimation of preferring one of his anterior bargains to the present!—The last is always his best hit—his "Cynthia of the minute."—Alas! how many a mild Madonna have I known to *come in*—a Raphael!—keep its ascendency for a few brief moons—then, after certain intermedial degradations, from the front drawing-room to the back ¡gallery, thence to the dark parlor—adopted in turn by each of the Carracci, under successive lowering ascriptions of filiation, mildly breaking its fall—consigned to the oblivious lumber-room, *go out* at last a Lucca Giordano, or plain Carlo Maratti!—which things when I beheld—musing upon the chances and mutabilities of fate below, hath made me to reflect upon the altered condition of great personages, or that woful Queen of Richard II.—

> "—set forth in pomp,
> She came adorned hither like sweet May,
> Sent back like Hallowmas, or short'st of day."

With great love for *you* J. E. hath but a limited sympathy with what you feel or do. He lives in a world of his own, and makes slender guesses at what passes in your mind. He never pierces the marrow of your habits. He will tell an old-established play-goer that Mr. Such-a-one, of So-and-so (naming one of the theatres), is a very lively comedian—as a piece of news! He advertised me but the other day of some pleasant green lanes which he had found out for me,

knowing me to be a great walker, in my own immediate
vicinity, who have haunted the identical spot any time
these twenty years! He has not much respect for that
class of feelings which goes by the name of sentimental.
He applies the definition of real evil to bodily sufferings
exclusively, and rejecteth all others as imaginary. He
is affected by the sight or the bare supposition of a
creature in pain to a degree which I have never witnessed out of womankind. A constitutional acuteness
to this class of sufferings may in part account for this.
The animal tribe in particular he taketh under his especial protection. A broken-winded or spur-galled horse
is sure to find an advocate in him. An overloaded ass
is his client forever. He is the apostle to the brute kind
—the never-failing friend of those who have none to
care for them. The contemplation of a lobster boiled or
eels skinned *alive* will wring him so that "all for pity he
could die." It will take the savor from his palate and the
rest from his pillow for days and nights. With the intense feeling of Thomas Clarkson, he wanted only the
steadiness of pursuit and unity of purpose of that "true
yoke-fellow with Time" to have effected as much for
the *Animal* as *he* hath done for the *Negro Creation*.
But my uncontrollable cousin is but imperfectly formed
for purposes which demand coöperation. He cannot
wait. His amelioration-plans must be ripened in a day.
For this reason he has cut but an equivocal figure in
benevolent societies and combinations for the alleviation
of human sufferings. His zeal constantly makes him to
outrun and put out his coadjutors. He thinks of reliev-
ing, while they think of debating. He was blackballed
out of a society for the Relief of —— because the fervor
of his humanity toiled beyond the formal apprehension

and creeping processes of his associates. I shall always
consider this distinction as a patent of nobility in the
Elia family !

Do I mention these seeming inconsistencies to smile
at or upbraid my unique cousin? Marry, heaven, and
all good manners, and the understanding that should be
between kinsfolk, forbid !   With all the strangenesses of
this *strangest of the Elias*, I would not have him in one
jot or tittle other than he is; neither would I barter or
exchange my wild kinsman for the most exact, regular,
and every way consistent kinsman breathing.

In my next, reader, I may perhaps give you some account of my cousin Bridget—if you are not already sur-
feited with cousins—and take you by the hand, if you
are willing to go with us, on an excursion which we
made a summer or two since, in search of *more cousins—*

"Through the green plains of pleasant Hertfordshire."

MACKERY END, IN HERTFORDSHIRE.

BRIDGET ELIA has been my housekeeper for many a
long year. I have obligations to Bridget extending beyond the period of memory. We house together, old
bachelor and maid, in a sort of double singleness, with
such tolerable comfort, upon the whole, that I, for one,
find in myself no sort of disposition to go out upon the
mountains, with the rash king's offspring, to bewail my
celibacy. We agree pretty well in our tastes and habits
—yet so, as " with a difference." We are generally in
harmony, with occasional bickerings—as it should be
among near relations. Our sympathies are rather un-

derstood than expressed; and once, upon my dissembling a tone in my voice more kind than ordinary, my cousin burst into tears, and complained that I was altered. We are both great readers in different directions. While I am hanging over (for the thousandth time) some passage in old Burton, or one of his strange contemporaries, she is abstracted in some modern tale or adventure, whereof our common reading-table is daily fed with assiduously fresh supplies. Narrative teases me. I have little concern in the progress of events. She must have a story—well, ill, or indifferently told, so there be life stirring in it, and plenty of good or evil accidents. The fluctuations of fortune in fiction, and almost in real life, have ceased to interest, or operate but dully upon me. Out-of-the-way humors and opinions—heads with some diverting twist in them—the oddities of authorship please me most. My cousin has a native disrelish of anything that sounds odd or *bizarre*. Nothing goes down with her that is quaint, irregular, or out of the road of common sympathy. She "holds Nature more clever." I can pardon her blindness to the beautiful obliquities of the Religio Medici; but she must apologize to me for certain disrespectful insinuations which she has been pleased to throw out latterly touching the intellectuals of a dear favorite of mine, of the last century but one—the thrice noble, chaste, and virtuous, but again somewhat fantastical, and original-brained, generous Margaret Newcastle.

It has been the lot of my cousin, oftener perhaps than I could have wished, to have had for her associates and mine freethinkers—leaders and disciples of novel philosophies and systems; but she neither wrangles with nor accepts their opinions. That which was good and

venerable to her when a child retains its authority over
her mind still.   She never juggles or plays tricks with
her understanding.

We are both of us inclined to be a little too positive,
and I have observed the result of our disputes to be almost
uniformly this—that in matters of fact, dates, and circumstances, it turns out that I was in the right, and my
cousin in the wrong.   But where we have differed upon
moral points; upon something proper to be done or let
alone; whatever heat of opposition or steadiness of con-
viction I set out with, I am sure always, in the long-run,
to be brought over to her way of thinking.

I must touch upon the foibles of my kinswoman with
a gentle hand, for Bridget does not like to be told of her
faults.   She hath an awkward trick (to say no worse of
it) of reading in company; at which times she will answer *yes* or *no* to a question, without fully understanding
its purport—which is provoking, and derogatory in the
highest degree to the dignity of the putter of the said
question.   Her presence of mind is equal to the most
pressing trials of life, but will sometimes desert her upon
trifling occasions.   When the purpose requires it, and is
a thing of moment, she can speak to it greatly; but in
matters which are not stuff of the conscience, she hath
been known sometimes to let slip a word less seasonably.

Her education in youth was not much attended to;
and she happily missed all that train of female garniture,
which passeth by the name of accomplishments.   She
was tumbled early, by accident or design, into a spacious
closet of good old English reading, without much selec-
tion or prohibition, and browsed at will upon that fair
and wholesome pasturage.   Had I twenty girls, they
should be brought up exactly in this fashion.   I know

not whether their chance in wedlock might not be diminished by it; but I can answer for it, that it makes (if the worst comes to the worst) most incomparable old maids.

In a season of distress, she is the truest comforter; but in the teasing accidents, and minor perplexities, which do not call out the *will* to meet them, she sometimes maketh matters worse by an excess of participation. If she does not always divide your trouble, upon the pleasanter occasions of life she is sure always to treble your satisfaction. She is excellent to be at a play with, or upon a visit; but best, when she goes a journey with you.

We made an excursion together a few summers since, into Hertfordshire, to beat up the quarters of some of our less-known relations in that fine corn-country.

The oldest thing I remember is Mackery End; or Mackarel End, as it is spelt, perhaps more properly, in some old maps of Hertfordshire; a farmhouse—delightfully situated within a gentle walk from Wheathampstead. I can just remember having been there, on a visit to a great-aunt, when I was a child, under the care of Bridget; who, as I have said, is older than myself by some ten years. I wish that I could throw into a heap the remainder of our joint existences; that we might share them in equal division. But that is impossible. The house was at that time in the occupation of a substantial yeoman, who had married my grandmother's sister. His name was Gladman. My grandmother was a Bruton, married to a Field. The Gladmans and the Brutons are still flourishing in that part of the country, but the Fields are almost extinct. More than forty years had elapsed since the visit I speak of; and, for the greater portion of

that period, we had lost sight of the other two branches
also. Who or what sort of persons inherited Mackery
End—kindred or strange folk—we were afraid almost to
conjecture, but determined some day to explore.

By somewhat a circuitous route, taking the noble
park at Luton in our way from Saint Albans, we arrived
at the spot of our anxious curiosity about noon. The
sight of the old farmhouse, though every trace of it was
effaced from my recollection, affected me with a pleasure
which I had not experienced for many a year. For
though *I* had forgotten it, *we* had never forgotten being
there together, and we had been talking about Mackery
End all our lives, till memory on my part became mocked
with a phantom of itself, and I thought I knew the aspect
of a place which, when present, O how unlike it was to
that which I had conjured up so many times instead
of it!

Still the air breathed balmily about it; the season
was in the "heart of June," and I could say with the
poet—

> "But thou, that didst appear so fair
>   To fond imagination,
>   Dost rival in the light of day
>   Her delicate creation!"

Bridget's was more a waking bliss than mine, for she
easily remembered her old acquaintance again—some
altered features, of course, a little grudged at. At first,
indeed, she was ready to disbelieve for joy; but the
scene soon reconfirmed itself in her affections—and she
traversed every outpost of the old mansion, to the wood-
house, the orchard, the place where the pigeon-house
had stood (house and birds had alike flown)—with a
breathless impatience of recognition, which was more

pardonable perhaps than decorous at the age of fifty-odd.
But Bridget in some things is behind her years.

The only thing left was to get into the house—and
that was a difficulty which to me singly would have
been insurmountable; for I am terribly shy in making
myself known to strangers and out-of-date kinsfolk.
Love, stronger than scruple, winged my cousin in without me; but she soon returned with a creature that
might have sat to a sculptor for the image of Welcome.
It was the youngest of the Gladmans; who, by marriage
with a Bruton, had become mistress of the old mansion.
A comely brood are the Brutons. Six of them, females,
were noted as the handsomest young women in the
county. But this adopted Bruton, in my mind, was better than they all—more comely. She was born too late
to have remembered me. She just recollected in early
life to have had her cousin Bridget once pointed out to
her, climbing a stile. But the name of kindred, and of
cousinship, was enough. Those slender ties, that prove
slight as gossamer in the rending atmosphere of a metropolis, bind faster, as we found it, in hearty, homely,
loving Hertfordshire. In five minutes we were as thoroughly acquainted as if we had been born and bred up
together; were familiar, even to the calling each other
by our Christian names. So Christians should call one
another. To have seen Bridget, and her—it was like the
meeting of the two scriptural cousins! There was a
grace and dignity, an amplitude of form and stature, answering to her mind, in this farmer's wife, which would
have shined in a palace—or so we thought it. We were
made welcome by husband and wife equally—we, and
our friend that was with us. I had almost forgotten him
—but B. F. will not so soon forget that meeting, if per-

adventure he shall read this on the far-distant shores
where the kangaroo haunts. The fatted calf was made
ready, or rather was already so, as if in anticipation of
our coming; and, after an appropriate glass of native
wine, never let me forget with what honest pride this
hospitable cousin made us proceed to Wheatbampstead,
to introduce us (as some new-found rarity) to her mother
and sister Gladmans, who did indeed know something
more of us, at a time when she almost knew nothing.
With what corresponding kindness we were received by
them also—how Bridget's memory, exalted by the occasion, warmed into a thousand half-obliterated recollections of things and persons to my utter astonishment,
and her own—and to the astoundment of B. F., who sat
by, almost the only thing that was not a cousin there—
old effaced images of more than half-forgotten names and
circumstances still crowding back upon her, as words
written in lemon come out upon exposure to a friendly
warmth—when I forget all this, then may my country
cousins forget me; and Bridget no more remember, that
in the days of weakling infancy I was her tender charge
—as I have been her care in foolish manhood since—in
those pretty pastoral walks, long ago, about Mackery
End, in Hertfordshire.

MODERN GALLANTRY.

In comparing modern with ancient manners, we are
pleased to compliment ourselves upon the point of gallantry; a certain obsequiousness, or deferential respect,
which we are supposed to pay to females, as females.

I shall believe that this principle actuates our conduct, when I can forget that, in the nineteenth century of the era from which we date our civility, we are but just beginning to leave off the very frequent practice of whipping females in public, in common with the coarsest male offenders.

I shall believe it to be influential, when I can shut my eyes to the fact that in England women are still occasionally—hanged.

I shall believe in it, when actresses are no longer subject to be hissed off a stage by gentlemen.

I shall believe in it, when Dorimant hands a fish-wife across the kennel; or assists the apple-woman to pick up her wandering fruit, which some unlucky dray has just dissipated.

I shall believe in it, when the Dorimants in humbler life, who would be thought in their way notable adepts in this refinement, shall act upon it in places where they are not known, or think themselves not observed—when I shall see the traveler for some rich tradesman part with his admired box-coat, to spread it over the defenseless shoulders of the poor woman, who is passing to her parish on the roof of the same stage-coach with him, drenched in the rain—when I shall no longer see a woman standing up in the pit of a London theatre, till she is sick and faint with the exertion, with men about her, seated at their ease, and jeering at her distress; till one, that seems to have more manners or conscience than the rest, significantly declares "she should be welcome to his seat, if she were a little younger and handsomer." Place this dapper warehouseman, or that rider, in a circle of their own female acquaintance, and you shall confess you have not seen a politer-bred man in Lothbury.

Lastly, I shall begin to believe that there is some such principle influencing our conduct, when more than one-half of the drudgery and coarse servitude of the world shall cease to be performed by women.

Until that day comes, I shall never believe this boasted point to be anything more than a conventional fiction; a pageant got up between the sexes, in a certain rank, and at a certain time of life, in which both find their account equally.

I shall be even disposed to rank it among the salutary fictions of life, when in polite circles I shall see the same attentions paid to age as to youth, to homely features as to handsome, to coarse complexions as to clear —to the woman, as she is a woman, not as she is a beauty, a fortune, or a title.

I shall believe it to be something more than a name, when a well-dressed gentleman in a well-dressed company can advert to the topic of *female old age* without exciting, and intending to excite, a sneer—when the phrases " antiquated virginity," and such a one has " overstood her market," pronounced in good company, shall raise immediate offense in man, or woman, that shall hear them spoken.

Joseph Paice, of Bread Street Hill, merchant, and one of the Directors of the South-Sea Company—the same to whom Edwards, the Shakespeare commentator, has addressed a fine sonnet—was the only pattern of consistent gallantry I have met with. He took me under his shelter at an early age, and bestowed some pains upon me. I owe to his precepts and example whatever there is of the man of business (and that is not much) in my composition. It was not his fault that I did not profit more. Though bred a Presbyterian, and brought up a merchant, he was the finest gentleman of his time.   He had not *one* system of attention to females in the drawing-room, and *another* in the shop, or at the stall.   I do not mean that he made no distinction.   But he never lost sight of sex, or overlooked it in the casualties of a disadvantageous situation.   I have seen him stand bareheaded—smile if you please—to a poor servant-girl, while she has been inquiring of him the way to some street—in such a posture of unforced civility, as neither to embarrass her in the acceptance, nor himself in the offer, of it.   He was no dangler, in the common acceptation of the word, after women; but he reverenced and upheld, in every form in which it came before him, *womanhood*.   I have seen him—nay, smile not—tenderly escorting a market-woman, whom he had encountered in a shower, exalting his umbrella over her poor basket of fruit, that it might receive no damage, with as much carefulness as if she had been a countess. To the reverend form of Female Eld he would yield the wall (though it were to an ancient beggar-woman) with more ceremony than we can afford to show our grandams.   He was the Preux Chevalier of Age; the Sir Calidore, or Sir Tristan, to those who have no Calidores or Tristans to defend them.   The roses, that had long faded thence, still bloomed for him in those withered and yellow cheeks.

He was never married, but in his youth he paid his addresses to the beautiful Susan Winstanley—old Winstanley's daughter, of Clapton—who, dying in the early days of their courtship, confirmed in him the resolution of perpetual bachelorship.   It was during their short courtship, he told me, that he had been one day treating his mistress with a profusion of civil speeches—the com-

mon gallantries—to which kind of thing she had hitherto
manifested no repugnance—but in this instance with no
effect. He could not obtain from her a decent acknowl-
edgment in return. She rather seemed to resent his
compliments. He could not set it down to caprice, for
the lady had always shown herself above that littleness.
When he ventured on the following day, finding her a
little better humored, to expostulate with her on her
coldness of yesterday, she confessed, with her usual
frankness, that she had no sort of dislike to his attentions; that she could even endure some high-flown compliments; that a young woman placed in her situation had
a right to expect all sort of civil things said to her; that
she hoped she could digest a dose of adulation, short of
insincerity, with as little injury to her humility as most
young women; but that—a little before he had commenced his compliments—she had overheard him by
accident, in rather rough language, rating a young woman who had not brought home his cravats quite to the
appointed time, and she thought to herself, "As I am
Miss Susan Winstanley, and a young lady—a reputed
beauty, and known to be a fortune—I can have my choice
of the finest speeches from the mouth of this very fine
gentleman who is courting me—but if I had been poor
Mary Such-a-one (*naming the milliner*)—and had failed
of bringing home the cravats to the appointed hour—
though perhaps I had sat up half the night to forward
them—what sort of compliments should I have received
then?—And my woman's pride came to my assistance;
and I thought that, if it were only done to do *me* honor,
a female, like myself, might have received handsomer
usage; and I was determined not to accept any fine
speeches, to the compromise of that sex, the belonging

to which was, after all, my strongest claim and title to
them." I think the lady discovered both generosity, and
a just way of thinking, in this rebuke which she gave
her lover; and I have sometimes imagined that the uncommon strain of courtesy, which through life regulated
the actions and behavior of my friend toward all of
womankind indiscriminately, owed its happy origin to
this seasonable lesson from the lips of his lamented mistress.

I wish the whole female world would entertain the
same notion of these things that Miss Winstanley showed.
Then we should see something of the spirit of consistent
gallantry; and no longer witness the anomaly of the same
man—a pattern of true politeness to a wife—of cold
contempt, or rudeness, to a sister—the idolater of his female mistress—the disparager and despiser of his no less
female aunt, or unfortunate—still female—maiden cousin.
Just so much respect as a woman derogates from her own
sex, in whatever condition placed—her handmaid, or de-
pendent—she deserves to have diminished from herself
on that score; and probably will feel the diminution
when youth, and beauty, and advantages, not inseparable
from sex, shall lose of their attraction.   What a woman
should demand of a man in courtship, or after it, is first—
respect for her as she is a woman; and next to that—to
be respected by him above all other women.   But let her
stand upon her female character as upon a foundation;
and let the attentions, incident to individual preference,
be so many pretty additaments and ornaments—as many,
and as fanciful, as you please—to that main structure.
Let her first lesson be, with sweet Susan Winstanley—to
reverence her sex.

THE OLD BENCHERS OF THE INNER TEMPLE.

I WAS born, and passed the first seven years of my life, in the Temple. Its church, its halls, its gardens, its fountain, its river, I had almost said—for in those young years, what was this king of rivers to me but a stream that watered our pleasant places?—these are of my oldest recollections. I repeat, to this day, no verses to myself more frequently, or with kindlier emotion, than those of Spenser, where he speaks of this spot:

> " There when they came, whereas those bricky towers,
>   The which on Themmes brode aged back doth ride,
> Where now the studious lawyers have their bowers,
>   · There whylome wont the Temple knights to bide,
>   Till they decayed through pride."

Indeed, it is the most elegant spot in the metropolis. What a transition for a countryman visiting London for the first time—the passing from the crowded Strand or Fleet Street, by unexpected avenues, into its magnificent, ample squares, its classic green recesses! What a cheerful, liberal look hath that portion of it which, from three sides, overlooks the greater garden; that goodly pile

> "Of building strong, albeit of Paper hight,"

confronting with massy contrast, the lighter, older, more fantastically shrouded one, named of Harcourt, with the cheerful Crown-office Row (place of my kindly engendure), right opposite the stately stream, which washes the garden-foot with her yet scarcely trade-polluted waters, and seems but just weaned from her Twickenham Naiades! A man would give something to have been born in such places. What a collegiate aspect has that

fine Elizabethan hall, where the fountain plays, which I
have made to rise and fall, how many times!—to the astoundment of the young urchins, my contemporaries,
who, not being able to guess at its recondite machinery,
were almost tempted to hail the wondrous work as magic! What an antique air had the now almost effaced sun-
dials, with their moral inscriptions, seeming coevals with
that Time which they measured, and to take their reve-
lations of its flight immediately from heaven, holding
correspondence with the fountain of light! How would
the dark line steal imperceptibly on, watched by the
eye of childhood, eager to detect its movement, never
catched, nice as an evanescent cloud, or the first arrests
of sleep!

> "Ah! yet doth beauty like a dial-hand
> Steal from his figure, and no pace perceived!"

What a dead thing is a clock, with its ponderous em-
bowelments of lead and brass, its pert or solemn dull-
ness of communicatión, compared with the simple altar-
like structure and silent heart-language of the old dial!
It stood as the garden-god of Christian gardens. Why
is it almost everywhere vanished? If its business use
be superseded by more elaborate inventions, its moral
uses, its beauty, might have pleaded for its continuance.
It spoke of moderate labors, of pleasures not protracted
after sunset, of temperance and good hours. It was the
primitive clock, the horologe of the first world. Adam
could scarce have missed it in Paradise. It was the
measure appropriate for sweet plants and flowers to
spring by, for the birds to apportion their silver war-
blings by, for flocks to pasture and be led to fold by.
The shepherd "carved it out quaintly in the sun;" and,

turning philosopher by the very occupation, provided it
with mottoes more touching than tombstones. It was a
pretty device of the gardener, recorded by Marvell, who,
in the days of artificial gardening, made a dial out of
herbs and flowers. I must quote his verses a little
higher up, for they are full, as all his serious poetry
was, of a witty delicacy. They will not come in awkwardly, I hope, in a talk of fountains and sundials. He
is speaking of sweet garden-scenes :

> " What wondrous life is this I lead ?
> Ripe apples drop about my head.
> The luscious clusters of the vine
> Upon my mouth do crush their wine.
> The nectarine, and curious peach,
> Into my hands themselves do reach.
> Stumbling on melons as I pass,
> Insnared with flowers, I fall on grass.
> Meanwhile the mind, from pleasure less
> Withdraws into its happiness.
> The mind, that ocean, where each kind
> Does straight its own resemblance find ;
> Yet it creates, transcending these,
> Far other worlds and other seas ;
> Annihilating all that's made
> To a green thought in a green shade.
> Here at the fountain's sliding foot,
> Or at some fruit-tree's mossy root,
> Casting the body's vest aside,
> My soul into the boughs does glide ;
> There like a bird it sits and sings,
> Then whets and claps its silver wings,
> And, till prepared for longer flight,
> Waves in its plumes the various light.

How well the skillful gardener drew,
Of flowers and herbs, this dial new !
Where from above the milder sun
Does through a fragrant zodiac run :
And, as it works, the industrious bee
Computes its time as well as we.
How could such sweet and wholesome hours
Be reckoned but with herbs and flowers ? " *

The artificial fountains of the metropolis are, in like manner, fast vanishing. Most of them are dried up or bricked over. Yet, where one is left, as in that little green nook behind the South-Sea House, what a freshness it gives to the dreary pile ! Four little winged marble boys used to play their virgin fancies, spouting out ever-fresh streams from their innocent wanton lips, in the square of Lincoln's Inn, when I was no bigger than they were figured. They are gone, and the spring choked up. The fashion, they tell me, is gone by, and these things are esteemed childish. Why not, then, gratify children by letting them stand ? Lawyers, I suppose, were children once. They are awakening images to them at least. Why must everything smack of man and mannish ? Is the world all grown up ? Is childhood dead ? Or is there not in the bosoms of the wisest and the best some of the child's heart left, to respond to its earliest enchantments ? The figures were grotesque. Are the stiff-wigged living figures, that still flitter and chatter about that area, less Gothic in appearance ? Or is the splutter of their hot rhetoric one half so refreshing and innocent as the little cool, playful streams those exploded cherubs uttered ?

* From a copy of verses entitled " The Garden."

They have lately gothicized the entrance to the Inner Temple Hall, and the library front; to assimilate them, I suppose, to the body of the hall, which they do not at all resemble. What is become of the winged horse that stood over the former? a stately arms! And who has removed those frescoes of the Virtues, which Italianized the end of the Paper-buildings?—my first hint of allegory! They must account to me for these things, which I miss so greatly.

The terrace is, indeed, left, which we used to call the parade; but the traces are passed away of the footsteps which made its pavement awful! It is become common and profane. The old benchers had it almost sacred to themselves, in the fore-part of the day at least. They might not be sided or jostled. Their air and dress asserted the parade. You left wide spaces betwixt you when you passed them. We walk on even terms with their successors. The roguish eye of J——ll, ever ready to be delivered of a jest, almost invites a stranger to vie a repartee with it. But what insolent familiar durst have mated Thomas Coventry?—whose person was a quadrate, his step massy and elephantine, his face square as the lion's, his gait peremptory and path-keeping, indivertible from his way as a moving column, the scarecrow of his inferiors, the browbeater of equals and superiors, who made a solitude of children wherever he came, for they fled his insufferable presence as they would have shunned an Elisha bear. His growl was as thunder in their ears, whether he spake to them in mirth or in rebuke—his invitatory notes being, indeed, of all, the most repulsive and horrid. Clouds of snuff, aggravating the natural terrors of his speech, broke from each majestic nostril, darkening the air. He took it, not by pinches, but a palmful at once, diving for it under the mighty flaps of his old-fashioned waistcoat-pocket; his waistcoat red and angry, his coat dark rappee, tinctured by dye original, and by adjuncts, with buttons of obsolete gold. And so he paced the terrace.

By his side a milder form was sometimes to be seen; the pensive gentility of Samuel Salt. They were coevals, and had nothing but that and their benchership in common. In politics Salt was a Whig, and Coventry a stanch Tory. Many a sarcastic growl did the latter cast out—for Coventry had a rough, spinous humor—at the political confederates of his associate, which rebounded from the gentle bosom of the latter like cannonballs from wool. You could not ruffle Samuel Salt.

S. had the reputation of being a very clever man, and of excellent discernment in the chamber practice of the law. I suspect his knowledge did not amount to much. When a case of difficult disposition of money, testamentary or otherwise, came before him, he ordinarily handed it over with a few instructions to his man Lovel, who was a quick little fellow, and would dispatch it out of hand by the light of natural understanding, of which he had an uncommon share. It was incredible what repute for talents S. enjoyed by the mere trick of gravity. He was a shy man; a child might pose him in a minute—indolent and procrastinating to the last degree. Yet men would give him credit for vast application, in spite of himself. He was not to be trusted with himself with impunity. He never dressed for a dinner-party but he forgot his sword—they wore swords then—or some other necessary part of his equipage. Lovel had his eye upon him on all these occasions, and ordinarily gave him his cue. If there was anything which he could speak unseasonably, he was sure to do it. He was to dine at a relative's of the unfortunate Miss Blandy on the day of her execution—and L., who had a wary foresight of his probable hallucinations, before he set out, schooled him with great anxiety not in any possible manner to allude to her story that day. S. promised faithfully to observe the injunction. He had not been seated in the parlor, where the company was expecting the dinner-summons, four minutes, when, a pause in the conversation ensuing, he got up, looked out of window, and pulling down his ruffles—an ordinary motion with him—observed, "it was a gloomy day," and added, "Miss Blandy must be hanged by this time, I suppose." Instances of this sort were perpetual. Yet S. was thought by some of the greatest men of his time a fit person to be consulted, not alone in matters pertaining to the law, but in the ordinary niceties and embarrassments of conduct—from force of manner entirely. He never laughed. He had the same good fortune among the female world—was a known toast with the ladies, and one or two are said to have died for love of him—I suppose, because he never trifled or talked gallantry with them, or paid them, indeed, hardly common attentions. He had a fine face and person, but wanted, methought, the spirit that should have shown them off with advantage to the women. His eye lacked lustre. Not so thought Susan P——; who, at the advanced age of sixty, was seen, in the cold evening-time, unaccompanied, wetting the pavement of B——d Row, with tears that fell in drops which might be heard, because her friend had died that day—he, whom she had pursued with a hopeless passion for the last forty years—a passion, which years could not extinguish or abate; nor the

long-resolved, yet gently-enforced, puttings off of unre-
lenting bachelorhood dissuade from its cherished purpose. Mild Susan P——, thou hast now thy friend in
heaven!

Thomas Coventry was a cadet of the noble family of
that name. He passed his youth in contracted circumstances, which gave him early those parsimonious habits
which in after-life never forsook him; so that, with one
windfall or another, about the time I knew him he was
master of four or five hundred thousand pounds; nor
did he look, or walk, worth a moidore less. He lived
in a gloomy house opposite the pump in Serjeant's Inn,
Fleet Street. J., the counsel, is doing self-imposed penance in it, for what reason I divine not, at this day. C.
had an agreeable seat at North Cray, where he seldom
spent above a day or two at a time in the summer; but
preferred, during the hot months, standing at his window in this damp, close, well-like mansion, to watch, as
he said, "the maids drawing water all day long." I suspect he had his within-door reasons for the preference.
Hic currus et arma fuêre. He might think his treasures
more safe. His house had the aspect of a strong-box.
C. was a close hunks—a hoarder rather than a miser—
or, if a miser, none of the mad Elwes breed, who have
brought discredit upon a character, which cannot exist
without certain admirable points of steadiness and unity
of purpose. One may hate a true miser, but cannot, I
suspect, so easily despise him. By taking care of the
pence, he is often enabled to part with the pounds, upon
a scale that leaves us careless, generous fellows halting
at an immeasurable distance behind. C. gave away
thirty thousand pounds at once in his lifetime to a blind
charity. His housekeeping was severely looked after,

but he kept the table of a gentleman. He would know
who came in and who went out of his house, but his
kitchen-chimney was never suffered to freeze.

Salt was his opposite in this, as in all—never knew
what he was worth in the world; and having but a
competency for his rank, which his indolent habits were
little calculated to improve, might have suffered severely
if he had not had honest people about him. Lovel took
care of everything. He was at once his clerk, his good
servant, his dresser, his friend, his "flapper," his guide,
stop-watch, auditor, treasurer. He did nothing without
consulting Lovel, or failed in anything without expecting and fearing his admonishing. He put himself almost
too much in his hands, had they not been the purest in
the world. He resigned his title almost to respect as a
master, if L. could ever have forgotten for a moment
that he was a servant.

I knew this Lovel. He was a man of an incorrigible
and losing honesty. A good fellow withal, and "would
strike." In the cause of the oppressed he never considered inequalities, or calculated the number of his op-
ponents. He once wrested a sword out of the hand of
a man of quality that had drawn upon him; and pom-
meled him severely with the hilt of it. The swordsman
had offered insult to a female—an occasion upon which
no odds against him could have prevented the interference of Lovel. He would stand next day bareheaded to
the same person, modestly to excuse his interference—
for L. never forgot rank, where something better was
not concerned. L. was the liveliest little fellow breathing, had a face as gay as Garrick's, whom he was said
greatly to resemble (I have a portrait of him which con-
firms it), possessed a fine turn for humorous poetry—next

to Swift and Prior—moulded heads in clay or plaster of Paris to admiration, by the dint of natural genius merely; turned cribbage-boards, and such small cabinet toys to perfection; took a hand at quadrille or bowls with equal facility; made punch better than any man of his degree in England; had the merriest quips and conceits; and was altogether as brimful of rogueries and inventions as you could desire. He was a brother of the angle, moreover, and just such a free, hearty, honest companion as Mr. Izaak Walton would have chosen to go a-fishing with. I saw him in his old age and the decay of his faculties, palsy-smitten, in the last sad stage of human weakness—"a remnant most forlorn of what he was"— yet even then his eye would light up upon the mention of his favorite Garrick. He was greatest, he would say, in Bayes—"was upon the stage nearly throughout the whole performance, and as busy as a bee." At intervals, too, he would speak of his former life, and how he came up a little boy from Lincoln to go to service, and how his mother cried at parting with him, and how he returned, after some few years' absence, in his smart, new livery, to see her, and she blessed herself at the change, and could hardly be brought to believe that it was "her own bairn." And then, the excitement subsiding, he would weep, till I have wished that sad second-childhood might have a mother still to lay its head upon her lap. But the common mother of us all in no long time after received him gently into hers.

With Coventry, and with Salt, in their walks upon the terrace, most commonly Peter Pierson would join to make up a third. They did not walk linked arm-in-arm in those days—"as now our stout triumvirs sweep the streets"—but generally with both hands folded behind them for state, or with one at least behind, the other carrying a cane. P. was a benevolent but not a prepossessing man. He had that in his face which you could not term unhappiness; it rather implied an incapacity of being happy. His cheeks were colorless even to whiteness. His look was uninviting, resembling (but without his sourness) that of our great philanthropist. I know that he *did* good acts, but I could never make out what he *was.* Contemporary with these, but subordinate, was Daines Barrington—another oddity—he walked burly and square—in imitation, I think, of Coventry—howbeit he attained not to the dignity of his prototype. Nevertheless, he did pretty well, upon the strength of being a tolerable antiquarian, and having a brother a bishop. When the account of his year's treasurership came to be audited, the following singular charge was unanimously disallowed by the bench: "Item, disbursed Mr. Allen, the gardener, twenty shillings, for stuff to poison the sparrows, by my orders." Next to him was old Barton—a jolly negation, who took upon him the ordering of the bills of fare for the Parliament chamber, where the benchers dine—answering to the combination rooms at College—much to the easement of his less epicurean brethren. I know nothing more of him.—Then Read, and Twopeny—Read, good-humored and personable—Twopeny, good-humored, but thin, and felicitous in jests upon his own figure. If T. was thin, Wharry was attenuated and fleeting. Many must remember him (for he was rather of later date) and his singular gait, which was performed by three steps and a jump regularly succeeding. The steps were little efforts, like that of a child beginning to walk; the jump comparatively vigorous, as a foot to an inch. Where he learned this figure, or what oc-

casioned it, I could never discover. It was neither graceful in itself, nor seemed to answer the purpose any better than common walking. The extreme tenuity of his
frame, I suspect, set him upon it. It was a trial of pois-
ing. Twopeny would often rally him upon his leanness,
and hail him as brother Lusty; but W. had no relish
of a joke. His features were spiteful. I have heard that
he would pinch his cat's ears extremely, when anything
had offended him. Jackson—the omniscient Jackson he
was called—was of this period. He had the reputation
of possessing more multifarious knowledge than any man
of his time. He was the Friar Bacon of the less literate
portion of the Temple. I remember a pleasant passage,
of the cook applying to him, with much formality of
apology, for instructions how to write down *edge* bone
of beef in his bill of commons. He was supposed to
know, if any man in the world did. He decided the or-
thography to be—as I have given it—fortifying his authority with such anatomical reasons as dismissed the
manciple (for the time) learned and happy. Some do
spell it yet, perversely, *aitch* bone, from a fanciful resem-
blance between its shape and that of the aspirate so de-
nominated. I had almost forgotten Mingay with the iron
hand—but he was somewhat later. He had lost his right
hand by some accident, and supplied it with a grappling-
hook, which he wielded with a tolerable adroitness. I
detected the substitute, before I was old enough to reason whether it were artificial or not. I remember the
astonishment it raised in me. He was a blustering, loud-
talking person; and I reconciled the phenomenon to my
ideas as an emblem of power—somewhat like the horns
in the forehead of Michael Angelo's Moses. Baron Ma-
seres, who walks (or did till very lately) in the costume

of the reign of George II., closes my imperfect recollections of the old benchers of the Inner Temple.

Fantastic forms, whither are ye fled? Or, if the like of you exist, why exist they no more for me? Ye inexplicable, half-understood appearances, why comes in reason to tear away the preternatural mist, bright or gloomy, that enshrouded you? Why make ye so sorry a figure in my relation, who made up to me—to my childish eyes —the mythology of the Temple? In those days I saw gods, as "old men covered with a mantle," walking upon the earth. Let the dreams of classic idolatry perish— extinct be the fairies and fairy trumpery of legendary fabling, in the heart of childhood, there will, forever, spring up a well of innocent or wholesome superstition— the seeds of exaggeration will be busy there, and vital— from every-day forms educing the unknown and the uncommon. In that little Goshen there will be light, when the grown world flounders about in the darkness of sense and materiality. While childhood, and while dreams, reducing childhood, shall be left, Imagination shall not have spread her holy wings totally to fly the earth.

P. S.—I have done injustice to the soft shade of Samuel Salt. See what it is to trust to imperfect memory, and the erring notices of childhood! Yet I protest I always thought that he had been a bachelor! This gentleman, R. N. informs me, married young, and losing his lady in childbed, within the first year of their union, fell into a deep melancholy, from the effects of which, probably, he never thoroughly recovered. In what a new light does this place his rejection (oh, call it by a gentler name!) of mild Susan P——, unraveling into beauty certain peculiarities of this very shy and retiring character! Henceforth let no one receive the narratives

10

of Elia for true records! They are, in truth, but shadows of fact—verisimilitudes, not verities—or sitting but upon the remote edges and outskirts of history. He is no such honest chronicler as R. N., and would have done better, perhaps, to have consulted that gentleman, before he sent these incondite reminiscences to press. But the worthy sub-treasurer—who respects his old and his new masters—would but have been puzzled at the indecorous liberties of Elia. The good man wots not, peradventure, of the license which *Magazines* have arrived at in this plain-speaking age, or hardly dreams of their existence beyond the *Gentleman's*—his furthest monthly excursions in this nature having been long confined to the holy ground of honest *Urban's* obituary. May it be long before his own name shall help to swell those columns of unenvied flattery!—Meantime, O ye New Benchers of the Inner Temple, cherish him kindly, for he is himself the kindliest of human creatures. Should infirmities overtake him—he is yet in green and vigorous senility—make allowances for them, remembering that "ye yourselves are old." So may the Winged Horse, your ancient badge and cognizance, still flourish! so may future Hookers and Seldens illustrate your church and chambers! so may the sparrows, in default of more melodious quiristers, unpoisoned hop about your walks! so may the fresh-colored and cleanly nursery-maid, who, by leave, airs her playful charge in your stately gardens, drop her prettiest blushing curtsy as ye pass, reductive of juvenescent emotion! so may the younkers of this generation eye you, pacing your stately terrace, with the same superstitious veneration, with which the child Elia gazed on the Old Worthies that solemnized the parade before ye!

GRACE BEFORE MEAT.

THE custom of saying grace at meals had, probably, its origin in the early times of the world, and the hunter-state of man, when dinners were precarious things, and a full meal was something more than a common blessing! when a bellyful was a windfall, and looked like a special providence. In the shouts of triumphant songs with which, after a season of sharp abstinence, a lucky booty of deer's or goat's flesh would naturally be ushered home, existed, perhaps, the germ of the modern grace. It is not otherwise easy to be understood, why the blessing of food—the act of eating—should have had a particular expression of thanksgiving annexed to it, distinct from that implied and silent gratitude with which we are expected to enter upon the enjoyment of the many other various gifts and good things of existence.

I own that I am disposed to say grace upon twenty other occasions in the course of the day besides my dinner. I want a form for setting out upon a pleasant walk, for a moonlight ramble, for a friendly meeting, or a solved problem. Why have we none for books, those spiritual repasts—a grace before Milton—a grace before Shakespeare—a devotional exercise proper to be said before reading the "Fairy Queen?"—but the received ritual having prescribed these forms to the solitary ceremony of manducation, I shall confine my observations to the experience which I have had of the grace, properly so called; commending my new scheme for extension to a niche in the grand philosophical, poetical, and perchance in part heretical, liturgy, now compiling by my friend Homo Humanus, for the use of a certain snug congregation of Utopian Rabelaisian Christians, no matter where assembled.

The form, then, of the benediction before eating has its beauty at a poor man's table, or at the simple and un-provocative repast of children. It is here that the grace becomes exceedingly graceful. The indigent man, who hardly knows whether he shall have a meal the next day or not, sits down to his fare with a present sense of the blessing, which can be but feebly acted by the rich, into whose mind the conception of wanting a dinner could never, but by some extreme theory, have entered. The proper end of food—the animal sustenance—is barely contemplated by them. The poor man's bread is his daily bread, literally his bread for the day. Their courses are perennial.

Again, the plainest diet seems the fittest to be pre-ceded by the grace. That which is least stimulative to appetite, leaves the mind most free for foreign considera-tions. A man may feel thankful, heartily thankful, over a dish of plain mutton with turnips, and have leisure to reflect upon the ordinance and institution of eating; when he shall confess a perturbation of mind, incon-sistent with the purposes of the grace, at the presence of venison or turtle. When I have sate (a *rarus hospes*) at rich men's tables, with the savory soup and messes steaming up the nostrils, and moistening the lips of the guests with desire and a distracted choice, I have felt the introduction of that ceremony to be unseasonable. With the ravenous orgasm upon you, it seems imper-tinent to interpose a religious sentiment. It is a confu-sion of purpose to mutter out praises from a mouth that waters. The heats of epicurism put out the gentle flame of devotion. The incense which rises round is pagan, and the belly-god intercepts it for his own. The very excess of the provision beyond the needs, takes away all sense of proportion between the end and means. The giver is veiled by his gifts. You are startled at the injustice of returning thanks—for what?—for having too much, while so many starve. It is to praise the gods amiss.

I have observed this awkwardness felt, scarce consciously, perhaps, by the good man who says the grace. I have seen it in clergymen and others—a sort of shame —a sense of the co-presence of circumstances which unhallow the blessing. After a devotional tone put on for a few seconds, how rapidly the speaker will fall into his common voice! helping himself or his neighbor, as if to get rid of some uneasy sensation of hypocrisy. Not that the good man was a hypocrite, or was not most conscientious in the discharge of the duty; but he felt in his inmost mind the incompatibility of the scene and the viands before him, with the exercise of a calm and rational gratitude.

I hear somebody exclaim—Would you have Christians sit down at table, like hogs to their troughs, without remembering the Giver?—no—I would have them sit down as Christians, remembering the Giver, and less like hogs. Or if their appetites must run riot, and they must pamper themselves with delicacies for which East and West are ransacked, I would have them postpone their benediction to a fitter season, when appetite is laid; when the still, small voice can be heard, and the reason of the grace returns—with temperate diet and restricted dishes. Gluttony and surfeiting are no proper occasions for thanksgiving. When Jeshurun waxed fat, we read that he kicked. Virgil knew the harpy-nature better,

when he put into the mouth of Celæno anything but a
blessing. We may be gratefully sensible of the delicious-
ness of some kinds of food beyond others, though that is
a meaner and inferior gratitude: but the proper object
of the grace is sustenance, not relishes; daily bread, not
delicacies; the means of life, and not the means of pam-
pering the carcass. With what frame or composure, I
wonder, can a city chaplain pronounce his benediction at
some great Hall-feast, when he knows that his last con-
cluding pious word—and that in all probability, the sacred name which he preaches—is but the signal for so
many impatient harpies to commence their foul orgies,
with as little sense of true thankfulness (which is temperance) as those Virgilian fowl! It is well if the good
man himself does not feel his devotions a little clouded,
those foggy, sensuous steams mingling with and polluting
the pure altar-sacrifice.

The severest satire upon full tables and surfeits is the
banquet which Satan, in the "Paradise Regained," pro-
vides for a temptation in the wilderness:

> "A table richly spread in regal mode
> With dishes piled, and meats of noblest sort
> And savor; beasts of chase, or fowl of game,
> In pastry built, or from the spit, or boiled,
> Gris-amber-steamed; all fish from sea or shore,
> Freshet or purling brook, for which was drained
> Pontus, and Lucrine bay, and Afric coast."

The tempter, I warrant you, thought these cates
would go down without the recommendatory preface of
a benediction. They are like to be short graces where
the devil plays the host.—I am afraid the poet wants his
usual decorum in this place. Was he thinking of the

old Roman luxury, or of a gaudy day at Cambridge?
This was a temptation fitter for a Heliogabalus. The
whole banquet is too civic and culinary, and the accom-
paniments altogether a profanation of that deep, abstracted, holy scene. The mighty artillery of sauces,
which the cook-fiend conjures up, is out of proportion
to the simple wants and plain hunger of the guest. He
that disturbed him in his dreams, from his dreams might
have been taught better. To the temperate fantasies of
the famished Son of God, what sort of feasts presented
themselves?—He dreamed, indeed—

> "—As appetite is wont to dream,
>   Of meats and drinks, Nature's refreshment sweet."

But what meats?—

> " Him thought, he by the brook of Cherith stood,
>   And saw the ravens with their horny beaks
>   Food to Elijah bringing even and morn;
>   Though ravenous, taught to abstain from what they brought;
>   He saw the prophet also how he fled
>   Into the desert and how there he slept
>   Under a juniper; then how awaked
>   He found his supper on the coals prepared,
>   And by the angel was bid rise and eat,
>   And ate the second time after repose,
>   The strength whereof sufficed him forty days;
>   Sometimes, that with Elijah he partook,
>   Or as a guest with Daniel at his pulse."

Nothing in Milton is finelier fancied than these temperate
dreams of the divine Hungerer. To which of these two
visionary banquets, think you, would the introduction of
what is called the grace have been the most fitting and
pertinent?

Theoretically I am no enemy to graces; but practically I own that (before meat especially) they seem to involve something awkward and unseasonable. Our appetites, of one or another kind, are excellent spurs to our reason, which might otherwise but feebly set about the great ends of preserving and continuing the species. They are fit blessings to be contemplated at a distance with a becoming gratitude; but the moment of appetite (the judicious reader will apprehend me) is, perhaps, the least fit season for that exercise. The Quakers, who go about their business of every description with more calmness than we, have more title to the use of these benedictory prefaces. I have always admired their silent grace, and the more because I have observed their applications to the meat and drink following to be less passionate and sensual than ours. They are neither gluttons nor wine-bibbers as a people. They eat, as a horse bolts his chopped hay, with indifference, calmness, and cleanly circumstances. They neither grease nor slop themselves. When I see a citizen in his bib and tucker, I cannot imagine it a surplice.

I am no Quaker at my food. I confess I am not indifferent to the kinds of it. Those unctuous morsels of deer's flesh were not made to be received with dispassionate services. I hate a man who swallows it, affecting not to know what he is eating. I suspect his taste in higher matters. I shrink instinctively from one who professes to like minced veal. There is a physiognomical character in the tastes for food. C—— holds that a man cannot have a pure mind who refuses apple-dumplings. I am not certain but he is right. With the decay of my first innocence, I confess a less and less relish daily for those innocuous cates. The whole vegetable tribe have lost their gust with me. Only I stick to asparagus, which still seems to inspire gentle thoughts. I am impatient and querulous under culinary disappointments, as to come home at the dinner-hour, for instance, expecting some savory mess, and to find one quite tasteless and sapidless. Butter ill melted—that commonest of kitchen failures—puts me beside my tenor.—The author of the Rambler used to make inarticulate animal noises over a favorite food. Was this the music quite proper to be preceded by the grace? or would the pious man have done better to postpone his devotions to a season when the blessing might be contemplated with less perturbation? I quarrel with no man's tastes, nor would set my thin face against those excellent things, in their way, jollity and feasting. But as these exercises, however laudable, have little in them of grace or gracefulness, a man should be sure, before he ventures so to grace them, that while he is pretending his devotions otherwhere, he is not secretly kissing his hand to some great fish—his Dagon—with a special consecration of no ark but the fat tureen before him. Graces are the sweet preluding strains to the banquets of angels and children; to the roots and severer repasts of the Chartreuse; to the slender, but not slenderly acknowledged, refection of the poor and humble man; but at the heaped-up boards of the pampered and the luxurious they become of dissonant mood, less timed and tuned to the occasion, methinks, than the noise of those better befitting organs would be which children hear tales of, at Hog's Norton. We sit too long at our meals, or are too curious in the study of them, or too disordered in our application to them, or engross too great a portion of those good things (which should be common) to our share, to be able with any grace to say grace. To be thankful for what we grasp exceeding our proportion, is to add hypocrisy to injustice. A lurking sense of this truth is what makes the performance of this duty so cold and spiritless a service at most tables. In houses where the grace is as indispensable as the napkin, who has not seen that never-settled question arise, as to *who shall say it?* while the good man of the house and the visitor clergyman, or some other guest, belike of next authority, from years of gravity, shall be bandying about the office between them as a matter of compliment, each of them not unwilling to shift the awkward burden of equivocal duty from his own shoulders.

I once drank tea in company with two Methodist divines of different persuasions, whom it was my fortune to introduce to each other for the first time that evening. Before the first cup was handed round, one of these reverend gentlemen put it to the other, with all due solemnity, whether he chose to *say anything*. It seems it is the custom with some sectaries to put up a short prayer before this meal also. His reverend brother did not at first apprehend him, but, upon an explanation, with little less importance he made answer that it was not a custom known in his church: in which courteous evasion the other acquiescing for good manners' sake, or in compliance with a weak brother, the supplementary or tea-grace was waived altogether. With what spirit might not Lucian have painted two priests of *his* religion playing into each other's hands the compliment of performing or omitting a sacrifice—the hungry god meantime, doubtful of his incense, with expectant nostrils hovering over the two flamens, and (as between two stools) going away in the end without his supper!

A short form upon these occasions is felt to want reverence; a long one, I am afraid, cannot escape the charge of impertinence. I do not quite approve of the epigrammatic conciseness with which that equivocal wag (but my pleasant school-fellow) C. V. L., when importuned for a grace, used to inquire, first slyly leering down the table, "Is there no clergyman here?"—significantly adding, "Thank G—!" Nor do I think our old form at school quite pertinent, where we used to preface our bald bread-and-cheese suppers with a preamble, connecting with that humble blessing a recognition of benefits the most awful and overwhelming to the imagination which religion has to offer. *Non tunc illis erat locus.* I remember we were put to it to reconcile the phrase "good creatures," upon which the blessing rested, with the fare set before us, willfully understanding that expression in a low and animal sense—till some one recalled a legend, which told how, in the golden days of Christ's, the young Hospitallers were wont to have smoking joints of roast-meat upon their nightly boards, till some pious benefactor, commiserating the decencies, rather than the palates, of the children, commuted our flesh for garments, and gave us—*horresco referens*—trousers instead of mutton.

MY FIRST PLAY.

At the north end of Cross Court there yet stands a portal, of some architectural pretensions, though reduced to humble use, serving at present for an entrance to a printing-office. This old doorway, if you are young, reader, you may not know was the identical pit-entrance

to old Drury—Garrick's Drury—all of it that is left. I
never pass it without shaking some forty years from off
my shoulders, recurring to the evening when I passed
through it to see *my first play*. The afternoon had been
wet, and the condition of our going (the elder folks and
myself) was, that the rain should cease. With what a
beating heart did I watch from the window the pud-
dles, from the stillness of which I was taught to prog-
nosticate the desired cessation! I seem to remember
the last spurt, and the glee with which I ran to an-
nounce it.

We went with orders, which my godfather F. had
sent us. He kept the oil-shop (now Davies's) at the corner of Featherstone Buildings, in Holborn. F. was a
tall, grave person, lofty in speech, and had pretensions
above his rank. He associated in those days with John
Palmer, the comedian, whose gait and bearing he seemed
to copy; if John (which is quite as likely) did not rather
borrow somewhat of his manner from my godfather.
He was also known to, and visited by, Sheridan. It was
to his house in Holborn that young Brinsley brought his
first wife on her elopement with him from a boarding-
school at Bath—the beautiful Maria Linley. My parents
were present (over a quadrille table) when he arrived in
the evening with his harmonious charge. From either
of these connections, it may be inferred that my godfather could command an order for the then Drury Lane
Theatre at pleasure—and, indeed, a pretty liberal issue
of those cheap billets, in Brinsley's easy autograph, I
have heard him say was the sole remuneration which he
had received for many years' nightly illumination of the
orchestra and various avenues of that theatre—and he
was content it should be so. The honor of Sheridan's

familiarity—or supposed familiarity—was better to my godfather than money.

F. was the most gentlemanly of oilmen; grandiloquent, yet courteous. His delivery of the commonest matters of fact was Ciceronian. He had two Latin words almost constantly in his mouth (how odd sounds Latin from an oilman's lips!), which my better knowledge since has enabled me to correct. In strict pronunciation they should have been sounded *vice versâ*—but in those young years they impressed me with more awe than they would now do, read aright from Seneca or Varro —in his own peculiar pronunciation, monosyllabically elaborated, or Anglicized into something like *verse verse*. By an imposing manner, and the help of these distorted syllables, he climbed (but that was little) to the highest parochial honors which St. Andrew has to bestow.

He is dead—and thus much I thought due to his memory, both for my first orders (little wondrous talismans!—slight keys, and insignificant to outward sight, but opening to me more than Arabian paradises!) and, moreover, that by his testamentary beneficence I came into possession of the only landed property which I could ever call my own—situate near the roadway village of pleasant Puckeridge, in Hertfordshire. When I journeyed down to take possession, and planted foot on my own ground, the stately habits of the donor descended upon me, and I strode (shall I confess the vanity?) with larger paces over my allotment of three-quarters of an acre, with its commodious mansion in the midst, with the feeling of an English freeholder that all betwixt sky and centre was my own. The estate has passed into more prudent hands, and nothing but an agrarian can restore it.

In those days were pit orders. Beshrew the uncomfortable manager who abolished them!—with one of these we went. I remember the waiting at the door—not that which is left—but between that and an inner door in shelter—O when shall I be such an expectant again!—with the cry of nonpareils, an indispensable playhouse accompaniment in those days. As near as I can recollect, the fashionable pronunciation of the theatrical fruiteresses then was, "Chase some oranges, chase some numparels, chase a bill of the play"—chase *pro* chuse. But when we got in, and I beheld the green curtain that veiled a heaven to my imagination, which was soon to be disclosed—the breathless anticipations I endured! I had seen something like it in the plate prefixed to Troilus and Cressida, in Rowe's Shakespeare—the tent scene with Diomede—and a sight of that plate can always bring back in a measure the feeling of that evening. The boxes at that time, full of well-dressed women of quality, projected over the pit; and the pilasters reaching down were adorned with a glistering substance (I know not what) under glass (as it seemed), resembling—a homely fancy—but I judged it to be sugar-candy—yet, to my raised imagination, divested of its homelier qualities, it appeared a glorified candy! The orchestra lights at length arose, those "fair Auroras!" Once the bell sounded. It was to ring out yet once again—and, incapable of the anticipation, I reposed my shut eyes in a sort of resignation upon the maternal lap. It rang the second time. The curtain drew up. I was not past six years old, and the play was Artaxerxes!

I had dabbled a little in the Universal History—the ancient part of it—and here was the court of Persia. It was being admitted to a sight of the past. I took no

proper interest in the action going on, for I understood
not its import—but I heard the word Darius, and I was
in the midst of Daniel. All feeling was absorbed in
vision. Gorgeous vests, gardens, palaces, princesses,
passed before me. I knew not players. I was in Per-
sepolis for the time, and the burning idol of their devotion almost converted me into a worshiper. I was awe-
struck, and believed those significations to be something
more than elemental fires. It was all enchantment and
a dream. No such pleasure has since visited me but in
dreams—Harlequin's invasion followed; where, I remember, the transformation of the magistrates into reverend beldams seemed to me a piece of grave historic
justice, and the tailor carrying his own head to be as
sober a verity as the legend of St. Denys.

The next play to which I was taken was the Lady of
the Manor, of which, with the exception of some scenery,
very faint traces are left in my memory. It was followed
by a pantomime, called Lun's Ghost—a satiric touch, I
apprehend, upon Rich, not long since dead—but to my
apprehension (too sincere for satire), Lun was as remote
a piece of antiquity as Lud—the father of a line of Harlequins—transmitting his dagger of lath (the wooden
sceptre) through countless ages. I saw the primeval
Motley come from his silent tomb in a ghastly vest of
white patchwork, like the apparition of a dead rainbow.
So Harlequins (thought I) look when they are dead.

My third play followed in quick succession. It was
the Way of the World. I think I must have sat at it as
grave as a judge; for, I remember, the hysteric affectations of good Lady Wishfort affected me like some
solemn tragic passion. Robinson Crusoe followed; in
which Crusoe, man Friday, and the parrot, were as

good and authentic as in the story.   The clownery and
pantaloonery of these pantomimes have clean passed out
of my head.   I believe I no more laughed at them, than
at the same age I should have been disposed to laugh at
the grotesque Gothic heads (seeming to me then replete
with devout meaning) that· gape, and grin, in stone
around the inside of the old Round Church (my church)
of the Templars.

I saw these plays in the season 1781-'82, when I was
from six to seven years old.   After the intervention of
six or seven other years (for at school all play-going was
inhibited) I again entered the doors of a theatre.   That
old Artaxerxes evening had never done ringing in my
fancy.   I expected the same feelings to come again with
the same occasion.   But we differ from ourselves less at
sixty and sixteen, than the latter does from six.   In that
interval what had I not lost!   At the first period I knew
nothing, understood nothing, discriminated nothing.   I
felt all, loved all, wondered all—

> "Was nourished, I could not tell how—"

I had left the temple a devotee, and was returned a ra-
tionalist.   The same things were there materially; but
the emblem, the reference, was gone!   The green curtain was no longer a veil, drawn between two worlds,
the unfolding of which was to bring back past ages to
present a "royal ghost"—but a certain quantity of green
baize, which was to separate the audience for a given
time from certain of their fellow-men who were to come
forward and pretend those parts.   The lights—the or-
chestra-lights—came up a clumsy machinery.   The first
ring, and the second ring, was now but a trick of the
prompter's bell—which had been, like the note of the

cuckoo, a phantom of a voice, no hand seen or guessed at which ministered to its warning. The actors were men and women painted. I thought the fault was in them; but it was in myself, and the alteration which those many centuries—of six short twelvemonths—had wrought in me. Perhaps it was fortunate for me that the play of the evening was but an indifferent comedy, as it gave me time to crop some unreasonable expectations, which might have interfered with the genuine emotions with which I was soon after enabled to enter upon the first appearance to me of Mrs. Siddons in Isabella. Comparison and retrospection soon yielded to the present attraction of the scene; and the theatre became to me, upon a new stock, the most delightful of recreations.

DREAM-CHILDREN: A REVERIE.

CHILDREN love to listen to stories about their elders, when *they* were children; to stretch their imagination to the conception of a traditionary great-uncle or grandame, whom they never saw. It was in this spirit that my little ones crept about me the other evening to hear about their great-grandmother Field, who lived in a great house in Norfolk (a hundred times bigger than that in which they and papa lived) which had been the scene—so at least it was generally believed in that part of the country—of the tragic incidents which they had lately become familiar with from the ballad of the Children in the Wood. Certain it is that the whole story of the children and their cruel uncle was to be seen fairly carved out in wood upon the chimney-piece of the great hall,

11

the whole story down to the Robin Redbreasts! till a foolish rich person pulled it down to set up a marble one of modern invention in its stead, with no story upon it. Here Alice put out one of her dear mother's looks, too tender to be called upbraiding. Then I went on to say, how religious and how good their great-grandmother Field was, how beloved and respected by everybody, though she was not indeed the mistress of this great house, but had only the charge of it (and yet in some respects she might be said to be the mistress of it too) committed to her by the owner, who preferred living in a newer and more fashionable mansion which he had purchased somewhere in the adjoining county; but still she lived in it in a manner as if it had been her own, and kept up the dignity of the great house in a sort while she lived, which afterward came to decay, and was nearly pulled down, and all its old ornaments stripped and carried away to the owner's other house, where they were set up, and looked as awkward as if some one were to carry away the old tombs they had seen lately at the Abbey, and stick them up in Lady C.'s tawdry gilt drawing-room. Here John smiled, as much as to say, "That would be foolish indeed." And then I told how, when she came to die, her funeral was attended by a concourse of all the poor, and some of the gentry too, of the neighborhood for many miles round, to show their respect for her memory, because she had been such a good and religious woman, so good, indeed, that she knew all the Psaltery by heart, ay, and a great part of the Testament besides. Here little Alice spread her hands. Then I told what a tall, upright, graceful person their great-grandmother Field once was; and how in her youth she was esteemed the best dancer—here Alice's little right foot played an

involuntary movement, till, upon my looking grave, it
desisted—the best dancer, I was saying, in the county,
till a cruel disease, called a cancer, came, and bowed her
down with pain; but it could never bend her good spirits, or make them stoop, but they were still upright, because she was so good and religious.   Then I told how
she was used to sleep by herself in a lone chamber of the
great lone house, and how she believed that an apparition
of two infants was to be seen at midnight gliding up and
down the great staircase near where she slept, but she
said "Those innocents would do her no harm;" and how
frightened I used to be, though in those days I had my
maid to sleep with me, because I was never half so good
or religious as she—and yet I never saw the infants.
Here John expanded all his eyebrows and tried to look
courageous.   Then I told how good she was to all her
grandchildren, having us to the great house in the holidays, where I in particular used to spend many hours
by myself, in gazing upon the old busts of the twelve
Cæsars, that had been the Emperors of Rome, till the
old marble heads would seem to live again, or I to be
turned into marble with them; how I never could be
tired with roaming about that huge mansion, with its
vast empty rooms, with their worn-out hangings, fluttering tapestry, and carved oaken panels, with the gilding
almost rubbed out—sometimes in the spacious old-fashioned gardens, which I had almost to myself, unless when
now and then a solitary gardening-man would cross me
—and how the nectarines and peaches hung upon the
walls, without my ever offering to pluck them, because
they were forbidden fruit, unless now and then—and
because I had more pleasure in strolling about among
the old, melancholy-looking yew-trees, or the firs, and

picking up the red berries, and the fir-apples, which
were good for nothing but to look at—or in lying about
upon the fresh grass with all the fine garden smells around
me—or basking in the orangery, till I could almost fancy
myself ripening, too, along with the oranges and the
limes in that grateful warmth—or in watching the dace
that darted to and fro in the fish-pond, at the bottom of
the garden, with here and there a great sulky pike hanging midway down the water in silent state, as if it
mocked at their impertinent friskings — I had more
pleasure in these busy-idle diversions than in all the
sweet flavors of peaches, nectarines, oranges, and such-
like common baits of children. Here John slyly deposited back upon the plate a bunch of grapes, which, not
unobserved by Alice, he had meditated dividing with
her, and both seemed willing to relinquish them for the
present as irrelevant. Then, in somewhat a more heightened tone, I told how, though their great-grandmother
Field loved all her grandchildren, yet in an especial
manner she might be said to love their Uncle John
L——, because he was so handsome and spirited a youth,
and a king to the rest of us; and, instead of moping
about in solitary corners, like some of us, he would
mount the most mettlesome horse he could get, when
but an imp no bigger than themselves, and make it carry
him half over the county in a morning, and join the
hunters when there were any out—and yet he loved the
old great house and gardens too, but had too much spirit
to be always pent up within their boundaries—and how
their uncle grew up to man's estate as brave as he was
handsome, to the admiration of everybody, but of their
great-grandmother Field most especially; and how he
used to carry me upon his back when I was a lame-foot-

ed boy—for he was a good bit older than me—many a
mile when I could not walk for pain—and how in after-
life he became lame-footed too, and I did not always (I
fear) make allowances enough for him when he was impatient, and in pain, nor remember sufficiently how con-
siderate he had been to me when I was lame-footed;
and how, when he died, though he had not been dead
an hour, it seemed as if he had died a great while ago,
such a distance there is betwixt life and death: and
how I bore his death as I thought pretty well at first,
but afterward it haunted and haunted me; and though
I did not cry or take it to heart as some do, and as I
think he would have done if I had died, yet I missed
him all day long, and knew not till then how much I had
loved him. I missed his kindness, and I missed his cross-
ness, and wished him to be alive again, to be quarreling
with him (for we quarreled sometimes), rather than not
have him again, and was as uneasy without him, as he
their poor uncle must have been when the doctor took off
his limb.—Here the children fell a-crying, and asked if
their little mourning which they had on was not for Uncle
John, and they looked up and prayed me not to go on
about their uncle, but to tell them some stories about
their pretty dead mother. Then I told how for seven
long years, in hope sometimes, sometimes in despair, yet
persisting ever, I courted the fair Alice W—n; and, as
much as children could understand, I explained to them
what coyness, and difficulty, and denial, meant in maidens—when suddenly turning to Alice, the soul of the
first Alice looked out at her eyes with such a reality of
re-presentment, that I became in doubt which of them
stood there before me, or whose that bright hair was;
and while I stood gazing, both the children gradually

grew fainter to my view, receding, and still receding, till
nothing at last but too mournful features were seen in
the uttermost distance, which, without speech, strangely
impressed upon me the effects of speech: "We are not
of Alice, nor of thee, nor are we children at all. The
children of Alice call Bartrum father. We are nothing;
less than nothing, and dreams. We are only what might
have been, and must wait upon the tedious shores of
Lethe millions of ages before we have existence, and a
name"—and immediately awaking, I found myself quietly seated in my bachelor arm-chair, where I had fallen
asleep, with the faithful Bridget unchanged by my side—
but John L. (or James Elia) was gone forever.

DISTANT CORRESPONDENTS.

IN A LETTER TO B. F., ESQ., AT SYDNEY, NEW
SOUTH WALES.

MY DEAR F.: When I think how welcome the sight
of a letter from the world where you were born must be
to you in that strange one to which you have been trans-
planted, I feel some compunctious visitings at my long
silence. But, indeed, it is no easy effort to set about a
correspondence at our distance. The weary world of
waters between us oppresses the imagination. It is difficult to conceive how a scrawl of mine should ever stretch
across it. It is a sort of presumption to expect that
one's thoughts should live so far. It is like writing for
posterity; and reminds me of one of Mrs. Rowe's super-
scriptions, "Alcander to Strephon in the shades." Cow-

ley's Post-Angel is no more than would be expedient in such an intercourse. One drops a packet at Lombard Street, and in twenty-four hours a friend in Cumberland gets it as fresh as if it came in ice. It is only like whispering through a long trumpet. But suppose a tube let down from the moon, with yourself at one end, and *the man* at the other; it would be some balk to the spirit of conversation, if you knew that the dialogue exchanged with that interesting theosophist would take two or three revolutions of a higher luminary in its passage. Yet, for aught I know, you may be some parasangs nigher that primitive idea—Plato's man—than we in England here have the honor to reckon ourselves.

Epistolary matter usually compriseth three topics: news, sentiment, and puns. In the latter, I include all non-serious subjects; or subjects serious in themselves, but, treated after my fashion, non-seriously. And first, for news. In them the most desirable circumstance, I suppose, is that they shall be true. But what security can I have that what I now send you for truth shall not, before you get it, unaccountably turn into a lie? For instance, our mutual friend P. is at this present writing— *my. Now*—in good health, and enjoys a fair share of worldly reputation. You are glad to hear it. This is natural and friendly. But at this present reading—*your Now*—he may possibly be in the Bench, or going to be hanged, which in reason ought to abate something of your transport (i. e., at hearing he was well, etc.), or at least considerably to modify it. I am going to the play this evening to have a laugh with Munden. You have no theatre, I think you told me, in your land of d——d realities. You naturally lick your lips, and envy me my felicity. Think but a moment, and you will correct the

hateful emotion. Why is it Sunday morning with you,
and 1823? This confusion of tenses, this grand solecism of *two presents*, is in a degree common to all post-
age. But if I sent you word to Bath or Devizes, that I
was expecting the aforesaid treat this evening, though at
the moment you received the intelligence, my full feast
of fun would be over, yet there would be for a day or
two after, as you would well know, a smack, a relish
left upon my mental palate, which would give rational
encouragement for you to foster a portion at least of the
disagreeable passion which it was in part my intention
to produce. But, ten months hence, your envy or your
sympathy would be as useless as a passion spent upon
the dead. Not only does truth, in these long intervals,
un-essence herself, but (what is harder) one cannot vent-
ure a crude fiction, for the fear that it may ripen into a
truth upon the voyage. What a wild, improbable banter
I put upon you some three years since—of Will Weatherall having married a servant-maid! I remember gravely consulting you how we were to receive her—for Will's
wife was in no case to be rejected; and your no less serious replication in the matter; how tenderly you ad-
vised an abstemious introduction of literary topics before
the lady, with a caution not to be too forward in bringing on the carpet matters more within the sphere of her
intelligence; your deliberate judgment, or rather wise
suspension of sentence, how far jacks, and spits, and
mops, could with propriety be introduced as subjects;
whether the conscious avoiding of all such matters in
discourse would not have a worse look than the taking
of them casually in our way; in what manner we should
carry ourselves to our maid Becky, Mrs. William Weatherall being by; whether we should show more delicacy,

and a truer sense of respect for Will's wife, by treating
Becky with our customary chiding before her, or by an
unusual deferential civility paid to Becky as to a person
of great worth, but thrown by the caprice of fate into a
humble station.   There were difficulties, I remember, on
both sides, which you did me the favor to state with the
precision of a lawyer, united to the tenderness of a friend.
I laughed in my sleeve at your solemn pleadings, when
lo! while I was valuing myself upon this flam put upon you
in New South Wales, the devil in England, jealous possibly of any lie-children not his own or working after
my copy, has actually instigated our friend (not three
days since) to the commission of a matrimony, which
I had only conjured up for your diversion.   William
Weatherall has married Mrs. Cotterel's maid.   But to
take it in its truest sense, you will see, my dear F., that
news from me must become history to you; which I
neither profess to write, nor indeed care much for reading.   No person, under a diviner, can with any prospect
of veracity conduct a correspondence at such an arm's
length.   Two prophets, indeed, might thus interchange
intelligence with effect; the epoch of the writer (Ha-
bakkuk) falling in with the true present time of the re-
ceiver (Daniel); but, then, we are no prophets.

Then as to sentiment.   It fares little better with that.
This kind of dish, above all, requires to be served up
hot; or sent off in water-plates, that your friend may
have it almost as warm as yourself.   If it have time to
cool, it is the most tasteless of all cold meats.   I have
often smiled at a conceit of the late Lord O.   It seems
that, traveling somewhere about Geneva, he came to
some pretty green spot, or nook where a willow, or
something hung so fantastically and invitingly over a

stream—was it ?—or a rock ?—no matter—but the stillness and the repose, after a weary journey, 'tis likely, in
a languid moment of his Lordship's hot restless life, so
took his fancy that he could imagine no place so proper,
in the event of his death, to lay his bones in.   This was
all very natural and excusable as a sentiment, and shows
his character in a very pleasing light.   But when from
a passing sentiment it came to be an act; and when, by
a positive testamentary disposal, his remains were actually carried all that way from England ; who was there,
some desperate sentimentalists excepted, that did not
ask the question, Why could not his Lordship have found
a spot as solitary, a nook as romantic, a tree as green
and pendent, with a stream as emblematic to his purpose, in Surrey, in Dorset, or in Devon ?   Conceive the
sentiment boarded up, freighted, entered at the Custom-
House (startling the tide-waiters with the novelty),
hoisted into a ship.   Conceive it pawed about and handled between the rude jests of tarpaulin ruffians—a
thing of its delicate texture—the salt bilge wetting it till
it became as vapid as a damaged lustring.   Suppose it in
material danger (mariners have some superstition about
sentiments) of being tossed over in a fresh gale to some
propitiatory shark (spirit of Saint Gothard, save us from
a quietus so foreign to the deviser's purpose !) ; but it has
happily evaded a fishy consummation.   Trace it then to
its lucky landing—at Lyons shall we say ?—I have not
the map before me—jostled upon four men's shoulders—
baiting at this town—stopping to refresh at t'other village—waiting a passport here, a license there; the sanc-
tion of the magistracy in this district, the concurrence
of the ecclesiastics in that canton ; till at length it ar-
rives at its destination, tired out and jaded, from a brisk

sentiment, into a feature of silly pride, or tawdry senseless affectation. How few sentiments, my dear F., I am
afraid we can set down, in the sailor's phrase, as quite
sea-worthy!

Lastly, as to the agreeable levities, which, though
contemptible in bulk, are the twinkling corpuscula which
should irradiate a right friendly epistle—your puns and
small jests are, I apprehend, extremely circumscribed in
their sphere of action. They are so far from a capacity
of being packed up and sent beyond sea, they will
scarce endure to be transported by hand from this room
to the next. Their vigor is as the instant of their birth.
Their nutriment for their brief existence is the intellectual atmosphere of the by-standers: or this last is the
fine slime of Nilus—the *melior lutus*—whose maternal
recipiency is as necessary as the *sol pater* to their equivocal generation. A pun hath a hearty kind of present
ear-kissing smack with it: you can no more transmit it
in its pristine flavor, than you can send a kiss.—Have
you not tried in some instances to palm off a yesterday's
pun upon a gentleman, and has it answered? Not but it
was new to his hearing, but it did not seem to come new
from you. It did not hitch in. It was like picking up
at a village ale-house a two-days'-old newspaper. You
have not seen it before, but you resent the stale thing as
an affront. This sort of merchandise above all requires
a quick return. A pun, and its recognitory laugh, must
be co-instantaneous. The one is the brisk lightning, the
other the fierce thunder. A moment's interval, and the
link is snapped. A pun is reflected from a friend's face as
from a mirror. Who would consult his sweet visnomy,
if the polished surface were two or three minutes (not
to speak of twelve months, my dear F.) in giving back
its copy?

I cannot image to myself whereabout you are.
When I try to fix it, Peter Wilkins's island comes across
me. Sometimes you seem to be in the *Hades of Thieves.*
I see Diogenes prying among you with his perpetual
fruitless lantern. What must you be willing by this time
to give for the sight of an honest man! You must almost have forgotten how *we* look. And tell me, what
your Sydneyites do? are they th**v*ng all day long?
Merciful heaven! what property can stand against such
a depredation! The kangaroos—your Aborigines—do
they keep their primitive simplicity un-Europe-tainted,
with those little short fore-puds, looking like a lesson
framed by Nature to the pick-pocket! Marry, for diving into fobs they are rather lamely provided, *a priori;*
but if the hue-and-cry were once up, they would show as
fair a pair of hind-shifters as the expertest loco-motor in
the colony.—We hear the most improbable tales at this
distance. Pray is it true that the young Spartans among
you are born with six fingers, which spoils their scan-
ning?—It must look very odd; but use reconciles. For
their scansion, it is less to be regretted, for if they take
it into their heads to be poets, it is odds but they turn
out, the greater part of them, vile plagiarists.—Is there
much difference to see, too, between the son of a th**f,
and the grandson? or where does the taint stop? Do
you bleach in three or in four generations?—I have many
questions to put, but ten Delphic voyages can be made in
a shorter time than it will take to satisfy my scruples.—
Do you grow your own hemp?—What is your staple trade,
—exclusive of the national profession, I mean? Your
locksmiths, I take it, are some of your great capitalists.

I am insensibly chatting to you as familiarly as when
we used to exchange good-morrows out of our old con-

tiguous windows, in pump-famed Hare Court in the Temple. Why did you ever leave that quiet corner?—Why did I?—with its complement of four poor elms, from whose smoke-dyed barks, the theme of jesting ruralists, I picked my first lady-birds! My heart is as dry as that spring sometimes proves in a thirsty August, when I revert to the space that is between us; a length of passage enough to render obsolete the phrases of our English letters before they can reach you. But while I talk, I think you hear me—thoughts dallying with vain surmise—

> "Aye me! while thee the seas and sounding shores
> Hold far away."

Come back, before I am grown into a very old man, so as you shall hardly know me. Come, before Bridget walks on crutches. Girls whom you left children have become sage matrons while you are tarrying there. The blooming Miss W—r (you remember Sally W—r) called upon us yesterday, an aged crone. Folks, whom you knew, die off every year. Formerly, I thought that death was wearing out—I stood ramparted about with so many healthy friends. The departure of J. W., two springs back, corrected my delusion. Since then the old divorcer has been busy. If you do not make haste to return, there will be little left to greet you, of me, or mine.

THE PRAISE OF CHIMNEY-SWEEPERS.

I LIKE to meet a sweep—understand me—not a grown sweeper—old chimney-sweepers are by no means attractive—but one of those tender novices, blooming through their first nigritude, the maternal washings not quite effaced from the cheek—such as come forth with the dawn, or somewhat earlier, with their little professional notes sounding like the *peep peep* of a young sparrow; or liker to the matin lark should I pronounce them, in their aërial ascents not seldom anticipating the sunrise?

I have a kindly yearning toward these dim specks—poor blots—innocent blacknesses—

I reverence these young Africans of our own growth —these almost clergy imps, who sport their cloth without assumption; and from their little pulpits (the tops of chimneys), in the nipping air of a December morning, preach a lesson of patience to mankind.

When a child, what a mysterious pleasure it was to witness their operation! to see a chit no bigger than one's self, enter, one knew not by what process, into what seemed the *fauces Averni*—to pursue him in imagination, as he went sounding on through so many dark, stifling caverns, horrid shades!—to shudder with the idea that "now, surely, he must be lost forever!"—to revive at hearing his feeble shout of discovered daylight —and then (O fullness of delight!) running out-of-doors, to come just in time to see the sable phenomenon emerge in safety, the brandished weapon of his art victorious like some flag waved over a conquered citadel! I seem to remember having been told that a bad sweep was once left in a stack with his brush, to indicate which way the wind blew. It was an awful spectacle certainly; not much unlike the old stage direction in "Macbeth," where the "Apparition of a child crowned, with a tree in his hand, rises."

Reader, if thou meetest one of these small gentry in

thy early rambles, it is good to give him a penny. It is
better to give him twopence. If it be starving weather,
and to the proper troubles of his hard occupation, a pair
of kibed heels (no unusual accompaniment) be superadded, the demand on thy humanity will surely rise to a
tester.

There is a composition, the groundwork of which I
have understood to be the sweet wood 'yclept sassafras.
This wood boiled down to a kind of tea, and tempered
with an infusion of milk and sugar, hath to some tastes
a delicacy beyond the China luxury. I know not how
thy palate may relish it; for myself, with every deference to the judicious Mr. Read, who hath time out of
mind kept open a shop (the only one he avers in London)
for the vending of this " wholesome and pleasant bever-
age," on the south side of Fleet Street, as thou approach-
est Bridge Street — *the only Salopian house*—I have
never yet ventured to dip my own particular lip in a
basin of his commended ingredients—a cautious premo-
nition to the olfactories constantly whispering to me,
that my stomach must infallibly, with all due courtesy,
decline it. Yet I have seen palates, otherwise not
uninstructed in dietetical elegancies, sup it up with
avidity.

I know not by what particular conformation of the
organ it happens, but I have always found that this
composition is surprisingly gratifying to the palate of a
young chimney-sweeper — whether the oily particles
(sassafras is slightly oleaginous) do attenuate and soften
the fuliginous concretions, which are sometimes found
(in dissections) to adhere to the roof of the mouth in
these unfledged practitioners; or whether Nature, sensible that she had mingled too much of bitter wood in the

lot of these raw victims, caused to grow out of the earth her sassafras for a sweet lenitive—but so it is, that no possible taste or odor to the senses of a young chimney-sweeper can convey a delicate excitement comparable to this mixture. Being penniless, they will yet hang their black heads over the ascending steam, to gratify one sense if possible, seemingly no less pleased than those domestic animals—cats—when they purr over a new-found sprig of valerian. There is something more in these sympathies than philosophy can inculcate.

Now, albeit Mr. Read boasteth, not without reason, that his is the *only Salopian house;* yet be it known to thee, reader—if thou art one who keepest what are called good hours, thou art haply ignorant of the fact—he hath a race of industrious imitators, who from stalls, and under open sky, dispense the same savory mess to humbler customers, at that dead time of the dawn, when (as extremes meet) the rake, reeling home from his midnight cups, and the hard-handed artisan leaving his bed to resume the premature labors of the day, jostle, not unfrequently to the manifest disconcerting of the former, for the honors of the pavement. It is the time when, in summer, between the expired and the not yet relumined kitchen-fires, the kennels of our fair metropolis give forth their least satisfactory odors. The rake, who wisheth to dissipate his o'ernight vapors in more grateful coffee, curses the ungenial fume, as he passeth; but the artisan stops to taste, and blesses the fragrant breakfast.

This is *saloop*—the precocious herb-woman's darling —the delight of the early gardener, who transports his smoking cabbages by break of day from Hammersmith

to Covent Garden's famed piazzas—the delight, and oh!
I fear, too often the envy, of the unpennied sweep.
Him shouldst thou haply encounter, with his dim visage
pendent over the grateful steam, regale him with a
sumptuous basin (it will cost thee but three-halfpennies)
and a slice of delicate bread-and-butter (an added half-
penny)—so may thy culinary fires, eased of the o'er-
charged secretions from thy worse-placed hospitalities,
curl up a lighter volume to the welkin—so may the
descending soot never taint thy costly, well-ingredienced
soups—nor the odious cry, quick-reaching from street to
street, of the *fired chimney*, invite the rattling engines
from ten adjacent parishes, to disturb for a casual scin-
tillation thy peace and pocket!

I am by nature extremely susceptible of street af-
fronts; the jeers and taunts of the populace; the low-
bred triumph they display over the casual trip, or splashed
stocking of a gentleman.   Yet can I endure the joculari-
ty of a young sweep with something more than forgive-
ness.—In the last winter but one, pacing along Cheapside
with my accustomed precipitation when I walk westward,
a treacherous slide brought me upon my back in
an instant. I scrambled up with pain and shame enough
—yet outwardly trying to face it down, as if nothing had
happened—when the roguish grin of one of these young
wits encountered me.   There he stood, pointing me out
with his dusky finger to the mob, and to a poor woman
(I suppose his mother) in particular, till the tears, for the
exquisiteness of the fun (so he thought it), worked themselves out at the corners of his poor, red eyes, red from
many a previous weeping, and soot-inflamed, yet twinkling through all with such a joy, snatched out of desolation, that Hogarth —— but Hogarth has got him already

12

(how could he miss him?) in the March to Finchley, grinning at the pie-man—there he stood, as he stands in the picture, irremovable, as if the jest were to last for-ever—with such a maximum of glee, and minimum of mischief, in his mirth—for the grin of a genuine sweep hath absolutely no malice in it—that I could have been content, if the honor of a gentleman might endure it, to have remained his butt and his mockery till midnight.

I am by theory obdurate to the seductiveness of what are called a fine set of teeth. Every pair of rosy lips (the ladies must pardon me) is a casket presumably hold-ing such jewels; but, methinks, they should take leave to "air" them as frugally as possible. The fine lady, or fine gentleman, who show me their teeth, show me bones. Yet must I confess that, from the month of a true sweep a display (even to ostentation) of those white and shining ossifications, strikes me as an agreeable anomaly in man-ners, and an allowable piece of foppery. It is, as when

> "A sable cloud
> 　Turns forth her silver lining on the night."

It is like some remnant of gentry not quite extinct; a badge of better days; a hint of nobility—and doubtless, under the obscuring darkness and double night of their forlorn disguisement, oftentimes lurketh good blood, and gentle conditions, derived from lost ancestry, and a lapsed pedigree. The premature apprenticements of these tender victims give but too much encouragement, I fear, to clandestine and almost infantile abductions; the seeds of civility and true courtesy, so often discerni-ble in these young grafts (not otherwise to be accounted for) plainly hint at some forced adoptions; many noble Rachels mourning for their children, even in our days, countenance the fact; the tales of fairy-spiriting may shadow a lamentable verity, and the recovery of the young Montagu be but a solitary instance of good fortune out of many irreparable and hopeless *defiliations*.

In one of the state-beds at Arundel Castle, a few years since—under a ducal canopy—(that seat of the Howards is an object of curiosity to visitors, chiefly for its beds, in which the late duke was especially a connoisseur)—encircled with curtains of delicatest crimson, with starry coronets interwoven—folded between a pair of sheets whiter and softer than the lap where Venus lulled Ascanius—was discovered by chance, after all methods of search had failed, at noonday, fast asleep, a lost chimney-sweeper. The little creature, having somehow confounded his passage among the intricacies of those lordly chimneys, by some unknown aperture had alighted upon this magnificent chamber; and, tired with his tedious explorations, was unable to resist the delicious invitement to repose which he there saw exhibited; so, creeping between the sheets very quietly, laid his black head upon the pillow, and slept like a young Howard.

Such is the account given to the visitors at the Castle. —But I cannot help seeming to perceive a confirmation of what I have just hinted at in this story. A high instinct was at work in the case, or I am mistaken. Is it probable that a poor child of that description, with whatever weariness he might be visited, would have ventured, under such a penalty as he would be taught to expect, to uncover the sheets of a duke's bed, and deliberately to lay himself down between them, when the rug, or the carpet, presented an obvious couch, still far above his pretensions—is this probable, I would ask, if the great power of Nature, which I contend for, had not been

manifested within him, prompting to the adventure?
Doubtless this young nobleman (for such my mind mis-
gives me that he must be) was allured by some memory,
not amounting to full consciousness, of his condition in
infancy, when he was used to be lapped by his mother,
or his nurse, in just such sheets as he there found, into
which he was now but creeping back as into his proper
incunabula, and resting-place.—By no other theory than
by this sentiment of a preëxistent state (as I may call it),
can I explain a deed so venturous, and, indeed, upon any
other system so indecorous, in this tender, but unseasonable, sleeper.

My present friend, JEM WHITE, was so impressed with
a belief of metamorphoses like this frequently taking
place, that in some sort to reverse the wrongs of fortune
in these poor changelings, he instituted an annual feast
of chimney-sweepers, at which it was his pleasure to
officiate as host and waiter. It was a solemn supper,
held in Smithfield, upon the yearly return of the fair
of St. Bartholomew. Cards were issued a week before
to the master-sweeps in and about the metropolis, confining the invitation to their younger fry. Now and
then an elderly stripling would get in among us, and be
good-naturedly winked at; but our main body were
infantry. One unfortunate wight, indeed, who, relying
upon his dusky suit, had intruded himself into our
party, but, by tokens, was providentially discovered in
time to be no chimney-sweeper (all is not soot which
looks so), was quoited out of the presence with universal indignation, as not having on the wedding-gar-
ment; but in general the greatest harmony prevailed.
The place chosen was a convenient spot among the pens,
at the north side of the fair, not so far distant as to be

impervious to the agreeable hubbub of that vanity; but
remote enough not to be obvious to the interruption
of every gaping spectator in it. The guests assembled
about seven. In those little temporary parlors three
tables were spread with napery, not so fine as substantial, and at every board a comely hostess presided with
her pan of hissing sausages. The nostrils of the young
rogues dilated at the savor. James White, as head-
waiter, had charge of the first table; and myself, with
our trusty companion Bigod, ordinarily ministered to
the other two. There was clambering and jostling, you
may be sure, who should get at the first table—for Roch-
ester, in his maddest days, could not have done the humors of the scene with more spirit than my friend.
After some general expression of thanks for the honor
the company had done him, his inaugural ceremony was
to clasp the greasy waist of old Dame Ursula (the fattest
of the three), that stood frying and fretting, half-blessing,
half-cursing "the gentleman," and imprint upon her
chaste lips a tender salute, whereat the universal host
would set up a shout that tore the concave, while hundreds of grinning teeth startled the night with their
brightness. Oh, it was a pleasure to see the sable younkers lick in the unctuous meat, with *his* more unctuous
sayings—how he would fit the tit-bits to the puny
mouths, reserving the lengthier links for the seniors—
how he would intercept a morsel even in the jaws of
some young desperado, declaring it "must to the pan
again to be browned, for it was not fit for a gentleman's
eating"—how he would recommend this slice of white
bread, or that piece of kissing-crust, to a tender juvenile,
advising them all to have a care of cracking their teeth,
which were their best patrimony—how genteelly he

would deal about the small ale, as if it were wine, naming the brewer, and protesting, if it were not good, he should lose their custom; with a special recommendation to wipe the lip before drinking. Then we had our toasts—"The King"—"The Cloth"—which, whether they understood or not, was equally diverting and flattering; and, for a crowning sentiment, which never failed, "May the Brush supersede the Laurel!" All these, and fifty other fancies, which were rather felt than comprehended by his guests, would be utter, standing upon tables, and prefacing every sentiment with a "Gentlemen, give me leave to propose so and so," which was a prodigious comfort to those young orphans; every now and then stuffing into his mouth (for it did not do to be squeamish on these occasions) indiscriminate pieces of those reeking sausages, which pleased them mightily, and was the savoriest part, you may believe, of the entertainment.

> "Golden lads and lasses must,
> As chimney-sweepers, come to dust."—

James White is extinct, and with him these suppers have long ceased. He carried away with him half the fun of the world when he died—of my world at least. His old clients look for him among the pens; and, missing him, reproach the altered feast of St. Bartholomew, and the glory of Smithfield departed forever.

A COMPLAINT OF THE DECAY OF BEGGARS

IN THE METROPOLIS.

THE all-sweeping besom of societarian reformation—your only modern Alcides's club to rid the time of its abuses—is uplift with many-handed sway to extirpate the last fluttering tatters of the bugbear MENDICITY from the metropolis. Scrips, wallets, bags—staves, dogs, and crutches—the whole mendicant fraternity, with all their baggage, are fast posting out of the purlieus of this eleventh persecution. From the crowded crossing, from the corners of streets and turnings of alleys, the parting Genius of Beggary is "with sighing sent."

I do not approve of this wholesale going to work, this impertinent crusado, or *bellum ad exterminationem*, proclaimed against a species. Much good might be sucked from these beggars.

They were the oldest and the honorablest form of pauperism. Their appeals were to our common nature; less revolting to an ingenious mind than to be a suppliant to the particular humors or caprice of any fellow-creature, or set of fellow-creatures, parochial or societarian. Theirs were the only rates uninvidious in the levy, ungrudged in the assessment.

There was a dignity springing from the very depth of their desolation; as to be naked is to be so much nearer to the being a man, than to go in livery.

The greatest spirits have felt this in their reverses; and when Dionysius from king turned schoolmaster, do we feel anything toward him but contempt? Could Vandyck have made a picture of him swaying a ferula for a sceptre which would have affected our minds with

the same heroic pity, the same compassionate admiration, with which we regard his Belisarius begging for an
obolum? Would the moral have been more graceful,
more pathetic?

The Blind Beggar in the legend—the father of pretty
Bessy—whose story doggerel rhymes and alehouse signs
cannot so degrade or attenuate, but that some sparks of
a lustrous spirit will shine through the disguisements—
this noble Earl of Cornwall (as indeed he was), and mem-
orable sport of fortune, fleeing from the unjust sentence
of his liege lord, stripped of all, and seated on the flower-
ing green of Bethnal, with his more fresh and springing
daughter by his side, illumining his rags and his beggary—would the child and parent have cut a better
figure, doing the honors of a counter, or expiating their
fallen condition upon the three-foot eminence of some
sempstering shop-board?

In tale or history, your beggar is ever the just an-
tipode to your king. The poets and romancical writers
(as dear Margaret Newcastle would call them), when
they would most sharply and feelingly paint a reverse
of fortune, never stop till they have brought down
their hero in good earnest to rags and the wallet.
The depth of the descent illustrates the height he
falls from. There is no medium which can be presented to the imagination without offense. There
is no breaking the fall. Lear, thrown from his palace,
must divest him of his garments, till he answer "mere
nature;" and Cresseid, fallen from a prince's love, must
extend her pale arms, pale with other whiteness than of
beauty, supplicating lazar alms with bell and clap-dish.

The Lucian wits knew this very well; and, with a
converse policy, when they would express scorn of great-

ness without the pity, they show us an Alexander in the shades cobbling shoes, or a Semiramis getting up foul linen.

How would it sound in song, that a great monarch had declined his affections upon the daughter of a baker! yet do we feel the imagination at all violated when we read the "true ballad," where King Cophetua woos the beggar-maid?

Pauperism, pauper, poor man, are expressions of pity, but pity alloyed with contempt. No one properly contemns a beggar. Poverty is a comparative thing, and each degree of it is mocked by its "neighbor grice." Its poor-rents and comings-in are soon summed up and told. Its pretenses to property are almost ludicrous. Its pitiful attempts to save excite a smile. Every scornful companion can weigh his trifle-bigger purse against it. Poor man reproaches poor man in the streets with impolitic mention of his condition, his own being a shade better, while the rich pass by and jeer at both. No rascally comparative insults a Beggar, or thinks of weighing purses with him. He is not in the scale of comparison. He is not under the measure of property. He confessedly hath none, any more than a dog or a sheep. No one twitteth him with ostentation above his means. No one accuses him of pride, or upbraideth him with mock humility. None jostle with him for the wall, or pick quarrels for precedency. No wealthy neighbor seeketh to eject him from his tenement. No man sues him. No man goes to law with him. If I were not the independent gentleman that I am, rather than I would be a retainer to the great, a led captain, or a poor relation, I would choose, out of the delicacy and true greatness of my mind, to be a Beggar.

Rags, which are the reproach of poverty, are the Beggar's robes, and graceful *insignia* of his profession, his tenure, his full dress, the suit in which he is expected to show himself in public. He is never out of the fashion, or limpeth awkwardly behind it. He is not required to put on court mourning. He weareth all colors, fearing none. His costume hath undergone less change than the Quaker's. He is the only man in the universe who is not obliged to study appearances. The ups and downs of the world concern him no longer. He alone continueth in one stay. The price of stock or land affecteth him not. The fluctuations of agricultural or commercial prosperity touch him not, or at worst but change his customers. He is not expected to become bail or surety for any one. No man troubleth him with questioning his religion or politics. He is the only free man in the universe.

The Mendicants of this great city were so many of her sights, her lions. I can no more spare them than I could the Cries of London. No corner of a street is complete without them. They are as indispensable as the Ballad-Singer; and in their picturesque attire as ornamental as the signs of old London. They were the standing morals, emblems, mementoes, dial-mottos, the spital sermons, the books for children, the salutary check and pauses to the high and rushing tide of greasy citizenry—

—" Look
Upon that poor and broken bankrupt there."

Above all, those old blind Tobits that used to line the wall of Lincoln's-Inn Garden, before modern fastidiousness had expelled them, casting up their ruined orbs to catch a ray of pity, and (if possible) of light, with their faithful Dog Guide at their feet—whither are they fled? or into what corners, blind as themselves, have they been driven, out of the wholesome air and sun-warmth? immersed between four walls, in what withering poorhouse do they endure the penalty of double darkness, where the chink of the dropped half-penny no more consoles their forlorn bereavement, far from the sound of the cheerful and hope-stirring tread of the passenger? Where hang their useless staves? and who will farm their dogs?—Have the overseers of St. L— caused them to be shot? or were they tied up in sacks, and dropped into the Thames, at the suggestion of B—, the mild rector of B——?

Well fare the soul of unfastidious Vincent Bourne, most classical, and, at the same time, most English of the Latinists!—who has treated of this human and quadrupedal alliance, this dog and man friendship, in the sweetest of his poems, the *Epitaphium in Canem*, or *Dog's Epitaph*. Reader, peruse it; and say, if customary sights, which would call up such gentle poetry as this, were of a nature to do more harm or good to the moral sense of the passengers through the daily thoroughfares of a vast and busy metropolis:

" Pauperis hic Iri requiesco Lyciscus, herilis,
　　Dum vixi, tutela vigil columenque senectæ,
　　Dux cæco fidus: nec, me ducente, solebat,
　　Prætenso hinc atque hinc baculo, per iniqua locorum
　　Incertam explorare viam; sed fila secutus,
　　Quæ dubios regerent, passûs, vestigia tuta
　　Fixit inoffenso gressu; gelidumque sedile
　　In nudo nactus saxo, quâ prætereuntium
　　Unda frequens confluxit, ibi miserisque tenebras

Lamentis, noctemque oculis ploravit obortam.
Ploravit nec frustra; obolum dedit alter et alter,
Queis corda et mentem indiderat natura benignam.
Ad latus interea jacui sopitus herile,
Vel mediis vigil in somnis; ad herilia jussa
Auresque atque animum arrectus, seu frustula amicè
Porrexit sociasque dapes, seu longa diei
Tædia perpessus, reditum sub nocte parabat,
    Hi mores, hæc vita fuit, dum fata sinebant,
Dum neque languebam morbis, nec inerte senectâ;
Quæ tandem obrepsit, veterique satellite cæcum
Orbavit doninum: prisci sed gratia facti
Ne tota intereat, longos delecta per annos,
Exiguum hunc Irus tumulum de cespite fecit,
Etsi inopis, non ingratæ, munuscula dextræ;
Carmine signavitque brevi, dominumque canemque
Quod memoret, fidumque canem dominumque benignum."

"Poor Irus' faithful wolf-dog here I lie,
That wont to tend my old blind master's steps,
His guide and guard: nor, while my service lasted
Had he occasion for that staff, with which
He new goes picking out his path in fear
Over the highways and crossings; but would plant,
Safe in the conduct of my friendly string,
A firm foot forward still, till he had reached
His poor seat on some stone, nigh where the tide
Of passers-by in thickest confluence flowed:
To whom with loud and passionate laments
From morn to eve his dark estate he wailed.
Nor wailed to all in vain: some here and there,
The well-disposed and good, their pennies gave.
I meantime at his feet obsequious slept;
Not all-asleep in sleep, but heart and ear
Pricked up at his least motion; to receive

At his kind hand my customary crumbs,
And common portion in his feast of scraps;
Or when night warned us homeward, tired and spent
With our long day and tedious beggary.
   These were my manners, this my way of life,
Till age and slow disease me overtook,
And severed from my sightless master's side.
But lest the grace of so good deeds should die,
Through tract of years in mute oblivion lost,
This slender tomb of turf hath Irus reared,
Cheap monument of no ungrudging hand,
And with short verse inscribed it, to attest,
In long and lasting union to attest,
The virtues of the Beggar and his Dog."

These dim eyes have in vain explored for some months past a well-known figure, or part of the figure of a man, who used to glide his comely upper half over the pavements of London, wheeling along with most ingenious celerity upon a machine of wood; a spectacle to natives, to foreigners, and to children. He was of a robust make, with a florid, sailor-like complexion, and his head was bare to the storm and sunshine. He was a natural curiosity, a speculation to the scientific, a prodigy to the simple. The infant would stare at the mighty man brought down to his own level. The common cripple would despise his own pusillanimity, viewing the hale stoutness, and hearty heart, of this half-limbed giant. Few but must have noticed him; for the accident, which brought him low, took place during the riots of 1780, and he has been a groundling so long. He seemed earth-born, an Antæus, and to suck in fresh vigor from the soil which he neighbored. He was a grand fragment; as good as an Elgin marble. The nature, which should have recruited his reft legs and thighs, was not lost, but only retired into his upper parts, and he was half a Hercules. I heard a tremendous voice thundering and growling, as before an earthquake, and casting down my eyes, it was this mandrake reviling a steed that had started at his portentous appearance. He seemed to want but his just stature to have rent the offending quad-ruped in shivers. He was as the man-part of a centaur, from which the horse-half had been cloven in some dire Lapithan controversy. He moved on, as if he could have made shift with yet half of the body portion which was left him. The *os sublime* was not wanting; and he threw out yet a jolly countenance upon the heavens. For-ty-and-two years had he driven this out-of-door trade, and now that his hair is grizzled in the service, but his good spirits no way impaired, because he is not content to exchange his free air and exercise for the restraints of a poor-house, he is expiating his contumacy in one of those houses (ironically christened) of Correction.

Was a daily spectacle like this to be deemed a nui-sance, which called for legal interference to remove? or not rather a salutary and a touching object, to the pass-ers-by in a great city? Among her shows, her museums, and supplies for ever-gaping curiosity (and what else but an accumulation of sights—endless sights—*is* a great city; or for what else is it desirable?) was there not room for one *Lusus* (not *Naturæ*, indeed, but) *Acciden-tium?* What if, in forty-and-two years' going about, the man had scraped together enough to give a portion to his child (as the rumor ran), of a few hundreds—whom had he injured?—whom had he imposed upon? The contributors had enjoyed their *sight* for their pennies. What if after being exposed all day to the heats, the rains, and the frosts of heaven—shuffling his ungainly trunk along in an elaborate and painful motion—he was enabled to retire at night to enjoy himself at a club of his fellow-cripples over a dish of hot meat and vegetables, as the charge was gravely brought against him by a clergyman deposing before a House of Commons' Committee—was *this*, or was his truly paternal consideration, which (if a fact) deserved a statue rather than a whipping-post, and is inconsistent at least with the exaggeration of nocturnal orgies which he has been slandered with—a reason that he should be deprived of his chosen, harmless, nay edifying, way of life, and be committed in hoary age for a sturdy vagabond?—

There was a Yorick once, whom it would not have shamed to have sate down at the cripples' feast, and to have thrown in his benediction, ay, and his mite, too, for a companionable symbol. "Age, thou hast lost thy breed."—

Half of these stories about the prodigious fortunes made by begging are (I verily believe) misers' calumnies. One was much talked of in the public papers some time since, and the usual charitable inferences deduced. A clerk in the Bank was surprised with the announcement of a five-hundred-pound legacy left him by a person whose name he was a stranger to. It seems that in his daily morning walks from Peckham (or some village thereabouts), where he lived, to his office, it had been his practice for the last twenty years to drop his halfpenny duly into the hat of some blind Bartimeus, that sate begging alms by the wayside in the Borough. The good old beggar recognized his daily benefactor by the voice only; and, when he died, left all the amassings of his alms (that had been half a century, perhaps, in the accu-

mulating) to his old Bank friend. Was this a story to
purse up people's hearts, and pennies, against giving an
alms to the blind?—or not rather a beautiful moral of
well-directed charity on the one part, and noble gratitude upon the other.

I sometimes wish I had been that Bank-clerk.

I seem ·to remember a poor, old, grateful kind of
creature, blinking, and looking up with his no eyes in
the sun—

Is it possible I could have steeled my purse against
him?

Perhaps I had no small change.

Reader, do not be frightened at the hard words, im-
position, imposture—*give, and ask no questions.* Cast
thy bread upon the waters. Some have, unawares (like
this Bank-clerk), entertained angels.

Shut not thy purse-strings always against painted distress. Act a charity sometimes. When a poor creature (outwardly and visibly such) comes before thee, do
not stay to inquire whether the "seven small children,"
in whose name he implores thy assistance, have a veri-
table existence. Rake not into the bowels of unwel-
come truth, to save a halfpenny. It is good to believe
him. If he be not all that he pretendeth, *give,* and
under a personate father of a family, think (if thou
pleasest) that thou hast relieved an indigent bachelor.
When they come with their counterfeit looks, and mumping tones, think them players. You pay your money to
see a comedian feign these things, which, concerning
these poor people, thou canst not certainly tell whether
they are feigned or not.

A DISSERTATION UPON ROAST-PIG.

MANKIND, says a Chinese manuscript, which my friend M. was obliging enough to read and explain to me, for the first seventy thousand ages ate their meat raw, clawing or biting it from the living animal, just as they do in Abyssinia to this day. This period is not obscurely hinted at by their great Confucius in the second chapter of his "Mundane Mutations," where he designates a kind of golden age by the term Cho-fang, literally the Cooks' Holiday. The manuscript goes on to say that the art of roasting, or rather broiling (which I take to be the elder brother) was accidentally discovered in the manner following: The swineherd, Ho-ti, having gone out into the woods one morning, as his manner was, to collect mast for his hogs, left his cottage in the care of his eldest son, Bo-bo, a great, lubberly boy, who, being fond of playing with fire, as younkers of his age commonly are, let some sparks escape into a bundle of straw, which, kindling quickly, spread the conflagration over every part of their poor mansion, till it was reduced to ashes. Together with the cottage (a sorry, antediluvian, makeshift of a building, you may think it), what was of much more importance, a fine litter of new-farrowed pigs, no less than nine in number, perished. China pigs have been esteemed a luxury all over the East, from the remotest periods that we read of. Bo-bo was in the utmost consternation, as you may think, not so much for the sake of the tenement, which his father and he could easily build up again with a few dry branches, and the labor of an hour or two, at any time, as for the loss of the pigs. While he was thinking

13

what he should say to his father, and wringing his hands over the smoking remnants of one of those untimely sufferers, an odor assailed his nostrils, unlike any scent which he had before experienced. What could it proceed from?—not from the burned cottage—he had smelt that smell before—indeed, this was by no means the first accident of the kind which had occurred through the negligence of this unlucky young fire-brand. Much less did it resemble that of any known herb, weed, or flower. A premonitory moistening at the same time overflowed his nether lip. He knew not what to think. He next stooped down to feel the pig, if there were any signs of life in it. He burned his fingers, and to cool them he applied them in his booby fashion to his mouth. Some of the crumbs of the scorched skin had come away with his fingers, and for the first time in his life (in the world's life, indeed, for before him no man had known it) he tasted—*crackling!* Again he felt and fumbled at the pig. It did not burn him so much now, still he licked his fingers from a sort of habit. The truth at length broke into his slow understanding that it was the pig that smelt so, and the pig that tasted so delicious; and surrendering himself up to the new-born pleasure, he fell to tearing up whole handfuls of the scorched skin with the flesh next it, and was cramming it down his throat in his beastly fashion, when his sire entered amid the smoking rafters, armed with retributory cudgel, and finding how affairs stood, began to rain blows upon the young rogue's shoulders, as thick as hailstones, which Bo-bo heeded not any more than if they had been flies. The tickling pleasure, which he experienced in his lower regions, had rendered him quite callous to any inconveniences he might feel in those remote quarters. His

father might lay on, but he could not beat him from his
pig, till he had fairly made an end of it, when, becoming
a little more sensible of his situation, something like the
following dialogue ensued:

"You graceless whelp, what have you got there de-
vouring? Is it not enough that you have burned me
down three houses with your dog's tricks, and be hanged
to you! but you must be eating fire, and I know not
what—what have you got there, I say?"

"O father, the pig, the pig! do come and taste how
nice the burnt pig eats!"

The ears of Ho-ti tingled with horror. He cursed
his son, and he cursed himself that ever he should beget
a son that should eat burnt pig.

Bo-bo, whose scent was wonderfully sharpened since
morning, soon raked out another pig, and fairly rending
it asunder, thrust the lesser half by main force into the
fists of Ho-ti, still shouting out, "Eat, eat, eat the burnt
pig, father, only taste—O Lord!"—with such-like bar-
barous ejaculations, cramming all the while as if he would
choke.

Ho-ti trembled every joint while he grasped the
abominable thing, wavering whether he should not put
his son to death for an unnatural young monster, when
the crackling scorching his fingers, as it had done his
son's, and applying the same remedy to them, he in his
turn tasted some of its flavor, which, make what sour
mouths he would for pretense, proved not altogether
displeasing to him. In conclusion (for the manuscript
here is a little tedious) both father and son fairly set
down to the mess, and never left off till they had dis-
patched all that remained of the litter.

Bo-bo was strictly enjoined not to let the secret escape, for the neighbors would certainly have stoned them for a couple of abominable wretches, who could think of improving upon the good meat which God had sent them. Nevertheless, strange stories got about. It was observed that Ho-ti's cottage was burnt down now more frequently than ever. Nothing but fires from this time forward. Some would break out in broad day, others in the night-time. As often as the sow farrowed, so sure was the house of Ho-ti to be in a blaze; and Ho-ti himself, which was the more remarkable, instead of chastising his son, seemed to grow more indulgent to him than ever. At length they were watched, the terrible mystery discovered, and father and son summoned to take their trial at Peking, then an inconsiderable assize town. Evidence was given, the obnoxious food itself produced in court, and verdict about to be pronounced, when the foreman of the jury begged that some of the burnt pig, of which the culprits stood accused, might be handed into the box. He handled it, and they all handled it; and burning their fingers, as Bo-bo and his father had done before them, and Nature prompting to each of them the same remedy, against the face of all the facts, and the clearest charge which judge had ever given—to the surprise of the whole court, townsfolk, strangers, reporters, and all present—without leaving the box, or any manner of consultation whatever, they brought in a simultaneous verdict of Not Guilty.

The judge, who was a shrewd fellow, winked at the manifest iniquity of the decision: and when the court was dismissed, went privily, and bought up all the pigs that could be had for love or money. In a few days his Lordship's town-house was observed to be on fire. The thing took wing, and now there was nothing to be seen but fire in every direction. Fuel and pigs grew enormously dear all over the district. The insurance-offices one and all shut up shop. People built slighter and slighter every day, until it was feared that the very science of architecture would, in no long time, be lost to the world. Thus this custom of firing houses continued, till in process of time, says my manuscript, a sage arose, like our Locke, who made a discovery, that the flesh of swine, or indeed, of any other animal, might be cooked (*burnt*, as they called it) without the necessity of consuming a whole house to dress it. Then first began the rude form of a gridiron. Roasting by the string or spit came in a century or two later, I forget in whose dynasty. By such slow degrees, concludes the manuscript, do the most useful, and seemingly the most obvious arts, make their way among mankind.—

Without placing too implicit faith in the account above given, it must be agreed that, if a worthy pretext for so dangerous an experiment as setting houses on fire (especially in these days) could be assigned in favor of any culinary object, that pretext and excuse might be found in ROAST-PIG.

Of all the delicacies in the whole *mundus edibilis*, I will maintain it to be the most delicate—*princeps obsoniorum*.

I speak not of your grown porkers—things between pig and pork—those hobbydehoys—but a young and tender suckling—under a moon old—guiltless, as yet, of the sty—with no original speck of the *amor immunditiæ*, the hereditary failing of the first parent, yet manifest—his voice, as yet, not broken, but something between a childish treble and a grumble—the mild forerunner, or *præludium* of a grunt.

He must be roasted. I am not ignorant that our ancestors ate them seethed, or boiled—but what a sacrifice of the exterior tegument!

There is no flavor comparable, I will contend, to that of the crisp, tawny, well-watched, not over-roasted, *crackling*, as it is well called—the very teeth are invited to their share of the pleasure at this banquet in overcoming the coy, brittle resistance—with the adhesive oleaginous—oh, call it not fat! but an indefinable sweetness growing up to it—the tender blossoming of fat—fat cropped in the bud—taken in the shoot—in the first innocence—the cream and quintessence of the child-pig's yet pure food——the lean, no lean, but a kind of animal manna—or rather, fat and lean (if it must be so) so blended and running into each other, that both together make but one ambrosian result, or common substance.

Behold him, while he is "doing"—it seemeth rather a refreshing warmth, than a scorching heat, that he is so passive to. How equably he twirleth round the string! —Now he is just done. To see the extreme sensibility of that tender age! he hath wept out his pretty eyes—radiant jellies—shooting-stars.—

See him in the dish, his second cradle, how meek he lieth!—wouldst thou have had this innocent grow up to the grossness and indocility which too often accompany maturer swinehood? Ten to one he would have proved a glutton, a sloven, an obstinate, disagreeable animal—wallowing in all manner of filthy conversation—from these sins he is happily snatched away—

> "Ere sin could blight or sorrow fade;
>   Death came with timely care—"

His memory is odoriferous—no clown curseth, while his

stomach half rejecteth, the rank bacon—no coal-heaver bolteth him in reeking sausages—he hath a fair sepulchre in the grateful stomach of the judicious epicure—and for such a tomb might be content to die.

He is the best of sapors. Pineapple is great. She is, indeed, almost too transcendent—a delight, if not sinful, yet so like to sinning that really a tender-conscienced person would do well to pause—too ravishing for mortal taste, she woundeth and excoriateth the lips that approach her—like lovers' kisses, she biteth—she is a pleasure bordering on pain from the fierceness and insanity of her relish—but she stoppeth at the palate—she meddleth not with the appetite—and the coarsest hunger might barter her consistently for a mutton-chop.

Pig—let me speak his praise—is no less provocative of the appetite, than he is satisfactory to the criticalness of the censorious palate. The strong man may batten on him, and the weakling refuseth not his mild juices.

Unlike to mankind's mixed characters, a bundle of virtues and vices, inexplicably intertwisted, and not to be unraveled without hazard, he is—good throughout. No part of him is better or worse than another. He helpeth, as far as his little means extend, all around. He is the least envious of banquets. He is all neighbors' fare.

I am one of those who freely and ungrudgingly impart a share of the good things of this life which fall to their lot (few as mine are in this kind) to a friend. I protest I take as great an interest in my friend's pleasures, his relishes, and proper satisfactions, as in mine own. "Presents," I often say, "endear Absents." Hares, pheasants, partridges, snipes, barn-door chickens (those "tame villatic fowl"), capons, plovers, brawn, barrels of oysters, I dispense as freely as I receive them. I love to taste them, as it were, upon the tongue of my friend. But a stop must be put somewhere. One would not, like Lear, "give everything." I make my stand upon pig. Methinks it is an ingratitude to the Giver of all good flavors, to extra-domiciliate, or send out of the house, slightingly (under pretext of friendship, or I know not what), a blessing so particularly adapted, predestined, I may say, to my individual palate. It argues an insensibility.

I remember a touch of conscience in this kind at school. My good old aunt, who never parted from me at the end of a holiday without stuffing a sweetmeat, or some nice thing, into my pocket, had dismissed me one evening with a smoking plum-cake, fresh from the oven. In my way to school (it was over London bridge) a gray-headed old beggar saluted me (I have no doubt, at this time of day, that he was a counterfeit). I had no pence to console him with, and in the vanity of self-denial, and the very coxcombry of charity, schoolboy-like, I made him a present of—the whole cake! I walked on a little, buoyed up, as one is on such occasions, with a sweet soothing of self-satisfaction; but before I had got to the end of the bridge, my better feelings returned, and I burst into tears, thinking how ungrateful I had been to my good aunt, to go and give her good gift away to a stranger that I had never seen before, and who might be a bad man for aught I knew; and then I thought of the pleasure my aunt would be taking in thinking that I—I myself, and not another—would eat her nice cake—and what should I say to her the next time I saw her—how naughty I was to part with her pretty present!—and the odor of that spicy cake came back upon my recollection, and the pleasure and the curiosity I had taken in seeing her make it, and her joy when she had sent it to the oven, and how disappointed she would feel that I had never had a bit of it in my mouth at last—and I blamed my impertinent spirit of alms-giving, and out-of-place hypocrisy of goodness ; and above all I wished never to see the face again of that insidious, good-for-nothing, old gray impostor.

Our ancestors were nice in their method of sacrificing these tender victims. We read of pigs whipped to death with something of a shock, as we hear of any other obsolete custom. The age of discipline is gone by, or it would be curious to inquire (in a philosophical light merely) what effect this process might have toward intenerating and dulcifying a substance naturally so mild and dulcet as the flesh of young pigs. It looks like refining a violet. Yet we should be cautious, while we condemn the inhumanity, how we censure the wisdom of the practice. It might impart a gusto.

I remember an hypothesis, argued upon by the young students, when I was at St. Omer's, and maintained with much learning and pleasantry on both sides, " Whether, supposing that the flavor of a pig who obtained his death by whipping (*per flaggellationem extremam*) superadded a pleasure upon the palate of a man more intense than any possible suffering we can conceive in the animal, is man justified in using that method of putting the animal to death ? " I forget the decision.

His sauce should be considered. Decidedly, a few bread-crumbs, done up with his liver and brains, and a dash of mild sage. But, banish, dear Mrs. Cook, I beseech you, the whole onion tribe. Barbecue your whole hogs to your palate, steep them in shalots, stuff them out with plantations of the rank and guilty garlic; you cannot poison them, or make them stronger than they are—but consider, he is a weakling—a flower.

A BACHELOR'S COMPLAINT OF THE BEHAVIOR OF MARRIED PEOPLE.

As a single man, I have spent a good deal of my time in noting down the infirmities of Married People, to console myself for those superior pleasures which they tell me I have lost by remaining as I am.

I cannot say that the quarrels of men and their wives ever made any great impression upon me, or had much tendency to strengthen me in those anti-social resolutions which I took up long ago upon more substantial considerations. What oftenest offends me at the houses of married persons where I visit, is an error of quite a different description—it is that they are too loving.

Not too loving neither: that does not explain my meaning. Besides, why should that offend me? The very act of separating themselves from the rest of the world, to have the fuller enjoyment of each other's society, implies that they prefer one another to all the world.

But what I complain of is, that they carry this preference so undisguisedly, they perk it up in the faces of us single people so shamelessly, you cannot be in their company a moment without being made to feel, by some indirect hint, or open avowal, that *you* are not the object of this preference. Now there are some things which give no offense, while implied or taken for granted

merely; but expressed, there is much offense in them.
If a man were to accost the first homely-featured or
plain-dressed young woman of his acquaintance, and tell
her bluntly that she was not handsome or rich enough
for him, and he could not marry her, he would deserve
to be kicked for his ill manners; yet no less is implied in
the fact that, having access and opportunity of putting
the question to her, he has never yet thought fit to do it.
The young woman understands this as clearly as if it
were put into words; but no reasonable young woman
would think of making this the ground of a quarrel.
Just as little right have a married couple to tell me by
speeches, and looks that are scarce less plain than speeches, that I am not the happy man—the lady's choice. It
is enough that I know I am not; I do not want this
perpetual reminding.

The display of superior knowledge or riches may be
made sufficiently mortifying; but these admit of a pal-
liative. The knowledge which is brought out to insult
me, may accidentally improve me; and in the rich man's
houses and pictures—his parks and gardens, I have a temporary usufruct at least. But the display of married
happiness has none of these palliatives; it is throughout
pure, unrecompensed, unqualified insult.

Marriage, by its best title, is a monopoly, and not of
the least invidious sort. It is the cunning of most pos-
sessors of any exclusive privilege to keep their advantage as much out of sight as possible, that their less
favored neighbors, seeing little of the benefit, may the
less be disposed to question the right. But these married monopolists thrust the most obnoxious part of their
patent into our faces.

Nothing is to me more distasteful than that entire

complacency and satisfaction which beam in the counte-
nances of a new-married couple—in that of the lady,
particularly: it tells you that her lot is disposed of in
this world; that *you* can have no hopes of her. It is
true, I have none; nor wishes either, perhaps; but this
is one of those truths which ought, as I said before, to
be taken for granted, not expressed.

The excessive airs which those people give themselves,
founded on the ignorance of us unmarried people, would
be more offensive if they were less irrational. We will
allow them to understand the mysteries belonging to
their own craft better than we, who have not had the
happiness to be made free of the company; but their
arrogance is not content within these limits. If a single
person presume to offer his opinion in their presence,
though upon the most indifferent subject, he is immediately silenced as an incompetent person. Nay, a young
married lady of my acquaintance, who, the best of the
jest was, had not changed her condition above a fortnight
before, in a question on which I had the misfortune to
differ from her, respecting the properest mode of breed-
ing oysters for the London market, had the assurance to
ask, with a sneer, how such an old Bachelor as I could
pretend to know anything about such matters!

But what I have spoken of hitherto is nothing to the
airs which these creatures give themselves when they
come, as they generally do, to have children. When I
consider how little of a rarity children are—that every
street and blind-alley swarms with them—that the poorest people commonly have them in most abundance—
that there are few marriages that are not blessed with at
least one of these bargains—how often they turn out ill,
and defeat the fond hopes of their parents, taking to

vicious courses, which end in poverty, disgrace, the gallows, etc.—I cannot for my life tell what cause for pride there can possibly be in having them. If they were young phœnixes, indeed, that were born but one in a year, there might be a pretext. But when they are so common—

I do not advert to the insolent merit which they assume with their husbands on these occasions. Let *them* look to that. But why *we*, who are not their natural-born subjects, should be expected to bring our spices, myrrh, and incense—our tribute and homage of admiration—I do not see.

"Like as the arrows in the hand of the giant even so are the young children;" so says the excellent office in our Prayer-book appointed for the churching of women. "Happy is the man that hath his quiver full of them;" so say I; but then don't let him discharge his quiver upon us that are weaponless—let them be arrows, but not to gall and stick us. I have generally observed that these arrows are double-headed; they have two forks, to be sure to hit with one or the other. As, for instance, where you come into a house which is full of children, if you happen to take no notice of them (you are thinking of something else, perhaps, and turn a deaf ear to their innocent caresses), you are set down as untractable, morose, a hater of children. On the other hand, if you find them more than usually engaging—if you are taken with their pretty manners, and set about in earnest to romp and play with them, some pretext or other is sure to be found for sending them out of the room: they are too noisy or boisterous, or Mr. —— does not like children. With one or other of these forks the arrow is sure to hit you.

I could forgive their jealousy, and dispense with toying with their brats, if it gives them any pain; but I think it unreasonable to be called upon to *love* them, where I see no occasion—to love a whole family, perhaps, eight, nine, or ten, indiscriminately—to love all the pretty dears, because children are so engaging!

I know there is a proverb, "Love me, love my dog;" that is not always so very practicable, particularly if the dog be set upon you to tease you or snap at you in sport. But a dog, or a lesser thing—any inanimate substance, as a keepsake, a watch, or a ring, a tree, or the place where we last parted when my friend went away upon a long absence, I can make shift to love, because I love him, and anything that reminds me of him; provided it be in its nature indifferent, and apt to receive whatever hue fancy can give it. But children have a real character, and an essential being of themselves; they are amiable or unamiable *per se;* I must love or hate them as I see cause for either in their qualities. A child's nature is too serious a thing to admit of its being regarded as a mere appendage to another being, and to be loved or hated accordingly; they stand with me upon their own stock, as much as men and women do. Oh! but you will say, sure it is an attractive age—there is something in the tender age of infancy that of itself charms us! That is the very reason why I am more nice about them. I know that a sweet child is the sweetest thing in Nature, not even excepting the delicate creatures which bear them; but the prettier the kind of thing is, the more desirable it is that it should be pretty of its kind. One daisy differs not much from another in glory; but a violet should look and smell the daintiest.—I was always rather squeamish in my women and children.

But this is not the worst: one must be admitted into their familiarity at least, before they can complain of inattention. It implies visits, and some kind of intercourse. But if the husband be a man with whom you have lived on a friendly footing before marriage—if you did not come in on the wife's side—if you did not sneak into the house in her train, but were an old friend in fast habits of intimacy before their courtship was so much as thought on—look about you—your tenure is precarious—before a twelvemonth shall roll over your head, you shall find your old friend gradually grow cool and altered toward you, and at last seek opportunities of breaking with you. I have scarce a married friend of my acquaintance, upon whose firm faith I can rely, whose friendship did not commence *after the period of his marriage.* With some limitations, they can endure that; but that the good man should have dared to enter into a solemn league of friendship in which they were not consulted, though it happened before they knew him—before they that are now man and wife ever met— this is intolerable to them. Every long friendship, every old authentic intimacy, must be brought into their office to be new stamped with their currency, as a sovereign prince calls in the good old money that was coined in some reign before he was born or thought of, to be new marked and minted with the stamp of his authority, before he will let it pass current in the world. You may guess what luck generally befalls such a rusty piece of metal as I am in these *new mintings.*

Innumerable are the ways which they take to insult and worm you out of their husband's confidence. Laughing at all you say with a kind of wonder, as if you were a queer kind of fellow that said good things, *but an oddity*, is one of the ways—they have a particular kind of stare for the purpose—till at last the husband, who used to defer to your judgment, and would pass over some excrescences of understanding and manner for the sake of a general vein of observation (not quite vulgar) which he perceived in you, begins to suspect whether you are not altogether a humorist—a fellow well enough to have consorted with in his bachelor days, but not quite so proper to be introduced to ladies. This may be called the staring way; and is that which has oftenest been put in practice against me.

Then there is the exaggerating way, or the way of irony; that is, where they find you an object of especial regard with their husband, who is not so easily to be shaken from the lasting attachment founded on esteem which he has conceived toward you, by never-qualified exaggerations to cry up all that you say or do, till the good man, who understands well enough that it is all done in compliment to him, grows weary of the debt of gratitude which is due to so much candor, and by relaxing a little on his part, and taking down a peg or two in his enthusiasm, sinks at length to the kindly level of moderate esteem—that "decent affection and complacent kindness" toward you, where she herself can join in sympathy with him without much stretch and violence to her sincerity.

Another way (for the ways they have to accomplish so desirable a purpose are infinite) is, with a kind of innocent simplicity, continually to mistake what it was which first made their husband fond of you. If an esteem for something excellent in your moral character was that which riveted the chain which she is to break upon any imaginary discovery of a want of poignancy in your conversation, she will cry, "I thought, my dear, you described your friend, Mr. ——, as a great wit?" If, on the other hand, it was for some supposed charm in your conversation that he first grew to like you, and was content for this to overlook some trifling irregularities in your moral deportment, upon the first notice of any of these she as readily exclaims, "This, my dear, is your good Mr. ——!" One good lady whom I took the liberty of expostulating with for not showing me quite so much respect as I thought due to her husband's old friend, had the candor to confess to me that she had often heard Mr. —— speak of me before marriage, and that she had conceived a great desire to be acquainted with me, but that the sight of me had very much disappointed her expectations; for from her husband's representations of me, she had formed a notion that she was to see a fine, tall, officer-like-looking man (I use her very words), the very reverse of which proved to be the truth. This was candid; and I had the civility not to ask her in return, how she came to pitch upon a standard of personal accomplishments for her husband's friends which differed so much from his own: for my friend's dimensions as near as possible approximate to mine; he standing five feet five in his shoes, in which I have the advantage of him by about half an inch; and he no more than myself exhibiting any indications of a martial character in his air or countenance.

These are some of the mortifications which I have encountered in the absurd attempt to visit at their houses. To enumerate them all would be a vain endeavor; I shall therefore just glance at the very common impropriety of which married ladies are guilty— of treating us as if we were their husbands, and *vice versa*.

14

I mean, when they use us with familiarity, and their
husbands with ceremony. *Testacea*, for instance, kept
me the other night two or three hours beyond my
usual time of supping, while she was fretting because Mr. —— did not come home till the oysters
were all spoiled, rather than she would be guilty of the
impoliteness of touching one in his absence.   This was
reversing the point of good manners; for ceremony is
an invention to take off the uneasy feeling which we derive from knowing ourselves to be less the object of love
and esteem with a fellow-creature than some other person is.   It endeavors to make up, by superior attentions
in little points, for that invidious preference which it is
forced to deny in the greater.   Had *Testacea* kept the
oysters back for me, and withstood her husband's im-
portunities to go to supper, she would have acted according to the strict rules of propriety.   I know no ceremony that ladies are bound to observe to their husbands,
beyond the point of a modest behavior and decorum;
therefore I must protest against the vicarious gluttony
of *Cerasia*, who at her own table sent away a dish of
Morellas, which I was applying to with great good-will,
to her husband at the other end of the table, and recom-
mended a plate of less extraordinary gooseberries to my
unwedded palate in their stead.   Neither can I excuse
the wanton affront of—

But I am weary of stringing up all my married acquaintance by Roman denominations.   Let them amend
and change their manners, or I promise to record the
full-length English of their names, to the terror of all
such desperate offenders in future.

ON SOME OF THE OLD ACTORS.

THE casual sight of an old play-bill, which I picked up the other day—I know not by what chance it was preserved so long—tempts me to call to mind a few of the players who make the principal figure in it.   It presents the cast of parts in the Twelfth Night, at the old Drury Lane Theatre two-and-thirty years ago.   There is something very touching in these old remembrances. They make us think how we *once* used to read a play-bill—not, as now, peradventure, singling out a favorite performer, and casting a negligent eye over the rest; but spelling out every name, down to the very mutes and servants of the scene—when it was a matter of no small moment to us whether Whitfield or Packer took the part of Fabian; when Benson, and Burton, and Phillimore—names of small account—had an importance beyond what we can be content to attribute now to the time's best actors.   "Orsino, by Mr. Barrymore."— What a full Shakespearean sound it carries! how fresh to memory arise the image and the manner of the gentle actor !

Those who have only seen Mrs. Jordan within the last ten or fifteen years can have no adequate notion of her performances of such parts as Ophelia; Helena, in All's Well that Ends Well; and Viola in this play.   Her voice had latterly acquired a coarseness which suited well enough with her Nells and Hoydens, but in those days it sank, with her steady, melting eye, into the heart.   Her joyous parts—in which her memory now chiefly lives—in her youth were outdone by her plaintive ones.   There is no giving an account how she delivered the disguised story of her love for Orsino. It was no set speech, that she had foreseen, so as to weave it into an harmonious period, line necessarily following line, to make up the music—yet I have heard it so spoken, or rather *read*, not without its grace and beauty — but, when she had declared her sister's history to be a "blank," and that she "never told her love," there was a pause, as if the story had ended—and then the image of the "worm in the bud" came up as a new suggestion—and the heightened image of "Patience" still followed after that, as by some growing (and not mechanical) process, thought springing up after thought, I would almost say, as they were watered by her tears. So in those fine lines—

> "Write loyal cantos of contemnèd love—
> Hollow your name to the reverberate hills "—

there was no preparation made in the foregoing image for that which was to follow. She used no rhetoric in her passion; or it was Nature's own rhetoric, most legitimate then, when it seemed altogether without rule or law. Mrs. Powel (now Mrs. Renard), then in the pride of her beauty, made an admirable Olivia. She was particularly excellent in her unbending scenes in conversation with the clown. I have seen some Olivias —and those very sensible actresses too—who in these interlocutions have seemed to set their wits at the jester, and to vie conceits with him in downright emulation. But she used him for her sport, like what he was, to trifle a leisure sentence or two with, and then to be dismissed, and she to be the great lady still. She touched the imperious, fantastic humor of the character with nicety. Her fine, spacious person filled the scene.

The part of Malvolio has, in my judgment, been so often misunderstood, and the *general merits* of the actor who then played it so unduly appreciated, that I shall hope for pardon if I am a little prolix upon these points.

Of all the actors who flourished in my time—a melancholy phrase if taken aright, reader—Bensley had most of the swell of soul, was greatest in the delivery of heroic conceptions, the emotions consequent upon the presentment of a great idea to the fancy. He had the true poetical enthusiasm—the rarest faculty among players. None that I remember possessed even a portion of that fine madness which he threw out in Hotspur's famous rant about glory, or the transports of the Venetian incendiary at the vision of the fired city. His voice had the dissonance, and at times the inspiriting effect, of the trumpet. His gait was uncouth and stiff, but no way embarrassed by affectation; and the thorough-bred gentleman was uppermost in every movement. He seized the moment of passion with greatest truth; like a faithful clock, never striking before the time; never anticipating or leading you to anticipate. He was totally destitute of trick and artifice. He seemed come upon the stage to do the poet's message simply, and he did it with as genuine fidelity as the nuncios in Homer deliver the errands of the gods. He let the passion or the sentiment do its own work without prop or bolstering. He would have scorned to mountebank it; and betrayed none of that *cleverness* which is the bane of serious acting. For this reason, his Iago was the only endurable one which I remember to have seen. No spectator from his action could divine more of his artifice than Othello was supposed to do. His confessions in soliloquy alone put you in possession of

the mystery. There were no by-intimations to make
the audience fancy their own discernment so much
greater than that of the Moor—who commonly stands
like a great helpless mark set up for mine ancient, and a
quantity of barren spectators, to shoot their bolts at.
The Iago of Bensley did not go to work so grossly.
There was a triumphant tone about the character, natural to a general consciousness of power; but none of
that petty vanity which chuckles and cannot contain itself upon any little successful stroke of its knavery—as
is common with your small villains and green probation-
ers in mischief. It did not clap or crow before its time.
It was not a man setting his wits at a child, and wink-
ing all the while at other children who are mightily
pleased at being let into the secret; but a consummate
villain entrapping a noble nature into toils, against which
no discernment was available, where the manner was as
fathomless as the purpose seemed dark, and without motive. The part of Malvolio, in the Twelfth Night, was
performed by Bensley, with a richness and a dignity,
of which (to judge from some recent castings of that
character) the very tradition must be worn out from the
stage. No manager in those days would have dreamed
of giving it to Mr. Baddeley, or Mr. Parsons: when
Bensley was occasionally absent from the theatre, John
Kemble thought it no derogation to succeed to the part.
Malvolio is not essentially ludicrous. He becomes comic
but by accident. He is cold, austere, repelling; but dig-
nified, consistent, and, for what appears, rather of an
overstretched morality. Maria describes him as a sort of
Puritan; and he might have worn his gold chain with
honor in one of our old Round-Head families, in the service of a Lambert or a Lady Fairfax. But his morality

and his manners are misplaced in Illyria. He is opposed to the proper *levities* of the piece, and falls in the unequal conquest. Still his pride, or his gravity (call it which you will), is inherent, and native to the man, not mock or affected, which latter only are the fit objects to excite laughter. His quality is at the best unlovely, but neither buffoon nor contemptible. His bearing is lofty, a little above his station, but probably not much above his deserts. We see no reason why he should not have been brave, honorable, accomplished. His careless committal of the ring to the ground (which he was commissioned to restore to Cesario), bespeaks a generosity of birth and feeling. His dialect on all occasions is that of a gentleman, and a man of education. We must not confound him with the eternal old, low steward of comedy. He is master of the household to a great princess; a dignity probably conferred upon him for other respects than age or length of service. Olivia, at the first indication of his supposed madness, declares that she " would not have him miscarry for half of her dowry." Does this look as if the character was meant to appear little or insignificant? Once, indeed, she accuses him to his face—of what?—of being " sick of self-love "—but with a gentleness and considerateness which could not have been, if she had not thought that this particular infirmity shaded some virtues. His rebuke to the knight and his sottish revelers is sensible and spirited; and when we take into consideration the unprotected condition of his mistress, and the strict regard with which her state of real or dissembled mourning would draw the eyes of the world upon her house-affairs, Malvolio might feel the honor of the family in some sort in his keeping; as it appears not that Olivia had any more brothers, or kinsmen, to look to it—for Sir Toby had dropped all such nice respects at the buttery-hatch. That Malvolio was meant to be represented as possessing estimable qualities, the expression of the duke, in his anxiety to have him reconciled, almost infers: "Pursue him, and entreat him to a peace." Even in his abused state of chains and darkness, a sort of greatness seems never to desert him. He argues highly and well with the supposed Sir Topas, and philosophizes gallantly upon his straw.* There must have been some shadow of worth about the man; he must have been something more than a mere vapor—a thing of straw, or Jack in office—before Fabian and Maria could have ventured sending him upon a courting-errand to Olivia. There was some consonancy (as he would say) in the undertaking, or the jest would have been too bold even for that house of misrule.

Bensley, accordingly, threw over the part an air of Spanish loftiness. He looked, spake, and moved, like an old Castilian. He was starch, spruce, opinionated, but his superstructure of pride seemed bottomed upon a sense of worth. There was something in it beyond the coxcomb. It was big and swelling, but you could not be sure that it was hollow. You might wish to see it taken down, but you felt that it was upon an elevation. He was magnificent from the outset; but when the decent

---

* *Clown.* What is the opinion of Pythagoras concerning wild fowl?

Mal. That the soul of our grandam might haply inhabit a bird.

Clown. What thinkest thou of his opinion?

Mal. I think nobly of the soul, and no way approve of his opinion.

sobrieties of the character began to give way, and the
poison of self-love, in his conceit of the countess's affection, gradually to work, you would have thought that
the hero of La Mancha in person stood before you.
How he went smiling to himself! with what ineffable
carelessness would he twirl his gold chain! what a
dream it was! you were infected with the illusion, and
did not wish that it should be removed! you had no room
for laughter! if an unseasonable reflection of morality
obtruded itself, it was a deep sense of the pitiable infirmity of man's nature, that can lay him open to such
frenzies—but in truth you rather admired than pitied
the lunacy while it lasted — you felt that an hour of
such mistake was worth an age with the eyes open.
Who would not wish to live but for a day in the conceit of such a lady's love as Olivia? Why, the Duke
would have given his principality but for a quarter of a
minute, sleeping or waking, to have been so deluded.
The man seemed to tread upon air, to taste manna, to
walk with his head in the clouds, to mate Hyperion.
Oh! shake not the castles of his pride—endure yet for a
season, bright moments of confidence—"stand still, ye
watches of the element," that Malvolio may be still in
fancy fair Olivia's lord!—but fate and retribution say no
—I hear the mischievous titter of Maria—the witty taunts
of Sir Toby—the still more insupportable triumph of the
foolish knight—the counterfeit Sir Topas is unmasked—
and "thus the whirligig of time," as the true clown hath
it, "brings in his revenges." I confess that I never saw
the catastrophe of this character, while Bensley played
it, without a kind of tragic interest. There was good
foolery too. Few now remember Dodd. What an Aguecheek the stage lost in him! Lovegrove, who came

nearest to the old actors, revived the character some few
seasons ago, and made it sufficiently grotesque; but Dodd
was *it*, as it came out of Nature's hands. It might be
said to remain *in puris naturalibus*. In expressing slow-
ness of apprehension, this actor surpassed all others.
You could see the first dawn of an idea stealing slowly
over his countenance, climbing up by little and little,
with a painful process, till it cleared up at last to the
fullness of a twilight conception—its highest meridian.
He seemed to keep back his intellect, as some have had
the power to retard their pulsation. The balloon takes
less time in filling, than it took to cover the expansion
of his broad, moony face over all its quarters with expression. A glimmer of understanding would appear in
a corner of his eye, and for lack of fuel go out again. A
part of his forehead would catch a little intelligence, and
be a long time in communicating it to the remainder.

I am ill at dates, but I think it is now better than
five-and-twenty years ago, that walking in the gardens
of Gray's Inn—they were then far finer than they are
now — the accursed Verulam Buildings had not en-
croached upon all the east side of them, cutting out delicate green crankles, and shouldering away one of two of
the stately alcoves of the terrace—the survivor stands
gaping and relationless as if it remembered its brother—
they are still the best gardens of any of the Inns of Court,
my beloved Temple not forgotten—have the gravest
character, their aspect being altogether reverend and
law-breathing—Bacon has left the impress of his foot
upon their gravel-walks—taking my afternoon solace
on a summer day upon the aforesaid terrace, a comely,
sad personage came toward me, whom, from his grave
air and deportment, I judged to be one of the old Bench-

ers of the Inn. He had a serious, thoughtful forehead, and seemed to be in meditations of mortality. As I have an instinctive awe of old Benchers, I was passing him with that sort of subindicative token of respect which one is apt to demonstrate toward a venerable stranger, and which rather denotes an inclination to greet him, than any positive motion of the body to that effect—a species of humility and will-worship which I observe, nine times out of ten, rather puzzles than pleases the person it is offered to—when the face turning full upon me, strangely identified itself with that of Dodd. Upon close inspection I was not mistaken. But could this sad, thoughtful countenance be the same vacant face of folly which I had hailed so often under circumstances of gayety; which I had never seen without a smile, or recognized but as the usher of mirth; that looked out so formally flat in Foppington, so frothily pert in Tattle, so impotently busy in Backbite; so blankly divested of all meaning, or resolutely expressive of none, in Acres, in Fribble, and a thousand agreeable impertinences? Was this the face—full of thought and carefulness—that had so often divested itself at will of every trace of either to give me diversion, to clear my cloudy face for two or three hours at least of its furrows? Was this the face—manly, sober, intelligent—which I had so often despised, made mocks at, made merry with? The remembrance of the freedoms which I had taken with it came upon me with a reproach of insult. I could have asked it pardon. I thought it looked upon me with a sense of injury. There is something strange as well as sad in seeing actors —your pleasant fellows particularly—subjected to and suffering the common lot; their fortunes, their casualties, their deaths, seem to belong to the scene, their actions to be amenable to poetic justice only. We can hardly connect them with more awful responsibilities. The death of this fine actor took place shortly after this meeting. He had quitted the stage some months; and, as I learned afterward, had been in the habit of resorting daily to these gardens almost to the day of his decease. In these serious walks probably he was divesting himself of many scenic and some real vanities—weaning himself from the frivolities of the lesser and the greater theatre —doing gentle penance for a life of no very reprehensible fooleries—taking off by degrees the buffoon mask, which he might feel he had worn too long—and rehearsing for a more solemn cast of part. Dying, he "put on the weeds of Dominic." *

If few can remember Dodd, many yet living will not easily forget the pleasant creature who in those days enacted the part of the Clown to Dodd's Sir Andrew.— Richard, or rather Dicky Suett—for so in his lifetime he delighted to be called, and time hath ratified the appellation—lies buried on the north side of the cemetery of Holy Paul, to whose service his nonage and tender years were dedicated. There are who do yet remember him at that period—his pipe clear and harmonious. He would

* Dodd was a man of reading, and left at his death a choice collection of old English literature. I should judge him to have been a man of wit. I know one instance of an impromptu which no length of study could have bettered. My merry friend, Jem White, had seen him one evening in Aguecheek, and recognizing Dodd the next day in Fleet Street, was irresistibly impelled to take off his hat and salute him as the identical Knight of the preceding evening with a " Save you, *Sir Andrew*." Dodd, not at all disconcerted at this unusual address from a stranger, with a courteous half-rebuking wave of the hand, put him off with an " Away, *Fool*."

often speak of his chorister days, when he was "cherub Dicky."

What clipped his wings, or made it expedient that he should change the holy for the profane state; whether he had lost his good voice (his best recommendation to that office) like Sir John, with "hallooing and singing of anthems;" or whether he was adjudged to lack something, even in those early years, of the gravity indispensable to an occupation which professeth to "commerce with the skies"—I could never rightly learn ; but we find him, after the probation of a twelvemonth or so, reverting to a secular condition, and become one of us.

I think he was not altogether of that timber out of which cathedral-seats and sounding-boards are hewed. But if a glad heart—kind, and therefore glad—be any part of sanctity, then might the robe of Motley, with which he invested himself with so much humility after his deprivation, and which he wore so long with so much blameless satisfaction to himself and to the public, be accepted for a surplice—his white stole and *albe*.

The first fruits of his secularization was an engagement upon the boards of Old Drury, at which theatre he commenced, as I have been told, with adopting the manner of Parsons in old men's characters. At the period in which most of us knew him, he was no more an imitator than he was in any true sense himself imitable.

He was the Robin Goodfellow of the stage. He came in to trouble all things with a welcome perplexity, himself no whit troubled for the matter. He was known, like Puck, by his note—*Ha! Ha! Ha!*—sometimes deepening to *Ho! Ho! Ho!* with an irresistible accession, derived, perhaps, remotely from his ecclesiastical education, foreign to his prototype of—*O La!* Thousands of hearts yet respond to the chuckling *O La!* of Dicky Suett, brought back to their remembrance by the faithful transcript of his friend Mathews's mimicry. The "force of nature could no further go." He drolled upon the stock of these two syllables richer than the cuckoo.

Care, that troubles all the world, was forgotten in his composition. Had he had but two grains (nay, half a grain) of it, he could never have supported himself upon those two spider's strings, which served him (in the latter part of his unmixed existence) as legs. A doubt or a scruple must have made him totter, a sigh have puffed him down; the weight of a frown had staggered him, a wrinkle made him lose his balance. But on he went, scrambling upon those airy stilts of his, with Robin Goodfellow, "thorough brake, thorough brier," reckless of a scratched face or a torn doublet.

Shakespeare foresaw him when he framed his fools and jesters. They have all the true Suett stamp, a loose and shambling gait, a slippery tongue, this last the ready midwife to a without-pain-delivered jest; in worlds light as air, venting truths deep as the centre; with idlest rhymes tagging conceit when busiest, singing with Lear in the tempest, or Sir Toby at the buttery-hatch.

Jack Bannister and he had the fortune to be more of personal favorites with the town than any actors before or after. The difference, I take it, was this: Jack was more *beloved* for his sweet, good-natured, moral pretensions. Dicky was more *liked* for his sweet, good-natured, no pretensions at all. Your whole conscience stirred with Bannister's performance of Walter in The Children in the Wood; but Dicky seemed like a thing,

as Shakespeare says of Love, too young to know what
conscience is. He put us into Vesta's days. Evil fled
before him—not as from Jack, as from an antagonist,
but because it could not touch him, any more than a
cannon-ball a fly. He was delivered from the burden
of that death; and, when death came himself, not in
metaphor, to fetch Dicky, it is recorded of him by
Robert Palmer, who kindly watched his exit, that he
received the last stroke, neither varying his accustomed
tranquillity, nor tune, with the simple exclamation,
worthy to have been recorded in his epitaph—*O La! O
La! Bobby!*

The elder Palmer (of stage-treading celebrity) commonly played Sir Toby in those days; but there is a
solidity of wit in the jests of that half-Falstaff which he
did not quite fill out. He was as much too showy as
Moody (who sometimes took the part) was dry and sottish. In sock or buskin there was an air of swaggering
gentility about Jack Palmer. He was a *gentleman* with
a slight infusion of *the footman*. His brother Bob (of
recenter memory), who was his shadow in everything
while he lived, and dwindled into less than a shadow
afterward—was a *gentleman* with a little stronger infusion of the *latter ingredient;* that was all. It is amazing
how a little of the more or less makes a difference in
these things. When you saw Bobby in the Duke's Servant,* you said, "What a pity such a pretty fellow was
only a servant!" When you saw Jack figuring in Captain Absolute, you thought you could trace his promotion to some lady of quality who fancied the handsome
fellow in his top-knot, and had bought him a commission.
Therefore Jack in Dick Amlet was insuperable.

* High Life Below Stairs.

Jack had two voices, both plausible, hypocritical, and insinuating; but his secondary or supplemental voice still more decisively histrionic than his common one. It was reserved for the spectator; and the *dramatis personæ* were supposed to know nothing at all about it. The *lies* of Young Wilding and the *sentiments* in Joseph Surface were thus marked out in a sort of italics to the audience. This secret correspondence with the company before the curtain (which is the bane and death of tragedy) has an extremely happy effect in some kinds of comedy, in the more highly artificial comedy of Congreve or of Sheridan especially, where the absolute sense of reality (so indispensable to scenes of interest) is not required, or would rather interfere to diminish your pleasure. The fact is, you do not believe in such characters as Surface—the villain of artificial comedy—even while you read or see them. If you did, they would shock and not divert you. When Ben, in Love for Love, returns from sea, the following exquisite dialogue occurs, at his first meeting with his father:

Sir Sampson. Thou hast been many a weary league, Ben, since I saw thee.

Ben. Ey, ey, been! Been far enough, an' that be all. Well, father, and how do all at home? how does brother Dick, and brother Val?

Sir Sampson. Dick! body o' me, Dick has been dead these two years. I writ you word when you were at Leghorn.

Ben. Mess, that's true; Marry, I had forgot. Dick's dead, as you say—well, and how?—I have a many questions to ask you.—

Here is an instance of insensibility which in real life would be revolting, or rather in real life could not have coexisted with the warm-hearted temperament of the character.   But when you read it in the spirit with which such playful selections and specious combinations rather than strict *metaphrases* of nature should be taken, or when you saw Bannister play it, it neither did, nor does, wound the moral sense at all.   For what is Ben— the pleasant sailor which Bannister gives us—but a piece of satire—a creation of Congreve's fancy—a dreamy combination of all the accidents of a sailor's character— his contempt of money—his credulity to women—with that necessary estrangement from home which it is just within the verge of credibility to suppose *might* produce such an hallucination as is here described?   We never think the worse of Ben for it, or feel it as a stain upon his character.   But when an actor comes, and instead of the delightful phantom—the creature dear to half-belief —which Bannister exhibited—displays before our eyes a downright concretion of a Wapping sailor—a jolly, warm-hearted Jack Tar—and nothing else—when instead of investing it with a delicious confusedness of the head, and a veering undirected goodness of purpose—he gives to it a downright daylight understanding, and a full consciousness of its actions; thrusting forward the sensibilities of the character with a pretense as if it stood upon nothing else, and was to be judged by them alone —we feel the discord of the thing; the scene is disturbed; a real man has got in among the *dramatis personæ*, and puts them out.   We want the sailor turned out.   We feel that his true place is not behind the curtain, but in the first or second gallery.

15   ———

ON THE ARTIFICIAL COMEDY OF THE LAST CENTURY.

THE artificial Comedy, or Comedy of manners, is quite extinct on our stage. Congreve and Farquhar show their heads once in seven years only, to be exploded and put down instantly. The times cannot bear them. Is it for a few wild speeches, an occasional license of dialogue? I think not altogether. The business of their dramatic characters will not stand the moral test. We screw everything up to that. Idle gallantry in a fiction, a dream, the passing pageant of an evening, startles us in the same way as the alarming indications of profligacy in a son or ward in real life should startle the parent or guardian. We have no such middle emotions as dramatic interests left. We see a stage libertine playing his loose pranks of two hours' duration, and of no after-consequence, with the severe eyes which inspect real vices with their bearings upon two worlds. We are spectators to a plot or intrigue (not reducible in life to the point of strict morality), and take it all for truth. We substitute a real for a dramatic person, and judge him accordingly. We try him in our courts, from which there is no appeal to the *dramatis personæ*, his peers. We have been spoiled with—not sentimental comedy—but a tyrant far more pernicious to our pleasures which has succeeded to it, the exclusive and all-devouring drama of common life; where the moral point is everything; where, instead of the fictitious half-believed personages of the stage (the phantoms of old comedy), we recognize ourselves, our brothers,

aunts, kinsfolk, allies, patrons, enemies—the same as in
life—with an interest in what is going on so hearty and
substantial, that we cannot afford our moral judgment,
in its deepest and most vital results, to compromise or
slumber for a moment. What is *there* transacting, by no
modification is made to affect us in any other manner
than the same events or characters would do in our
relationships of life. We carry our fireside concerns to
the theatre with us. We do not go thither, like our ancestors, to escape from the pressure of reality, so much
as to confirm our experience of it; to make assurance
double, and take a bond of fate. We must live our toilsome lives twice over, as it was the mournful privilege of
Ulysses to descend twice to the shades. All that neutral
ground of character, which stood between vice and virtue; or which in fact was indifferent to neither, where
neither properly was called in question; that happy
breathing-place from the burden of a perpetual moral
questioning—the sanctuary and quiet Alsatia of hunted
casuistry—is broken up and disfranchised, as injurious to
the interests of society. The privileges of the place are
taken away by law. We dare not dally with images, or
names, of wrong. We bark like foolish dogs at shadows.
We dread infection from the scenic representation of disorder, and fear a painted pustule. In our anxiety that
our morality should not take cold, we wrap it up in a
great blanket surtout of precaution against the breeze
and sunshine.

I confess for myself that (with no great delinquencies
to answer for) I am glad for a season to take an airing
beyond the diocese of the strict conscience—not to live
always in the precincts of the law-courts—but now and
then, for a dream-while or so, to imagine a world with

no meddling restrictions—to get into recesses, whither the hunter cannot follow me:

—" Secret shades
Of woody Ida's inmost grove,
While yet there was no fear of Jove."

I come back to my cage and my restraint the fresher and more healthy for it. I wear my shackles more contentedly for having respired the breath of an imaginary freedom. I do not know how it is with others, but I feel the better always for the perusal of ono of Congreve's— nay, why should I not add even of Wycherley's comedies. I am the gayer at least for it; and I could never connect those sports of a witty fancy in any shape with any result to be drawn from them to imitation in real life. They are a world of themselves almost as much as fairy-land. Take one their characters, male or female (with few exceptions they are alike), and place it in a modern play, and my virtuous indignation shall rise against the profligate wretch as warmly as the Oatos of the pit could desire; because in a modern play I am to judge of the right and the wrong. The standard of *police* is the measure of *political justice*. The atmosphere will blight it; it cannot live here. It has got into a moral world, where it has no business, from which it must needs fall headlong, as dizzy and incapable of making a stand as a Swedenborgian bad spirit that has wandered unawares into the sphere of one of his Good Men or Angels. But in its own world do we feel the creature is so very bad? The Fainalls and the Mirabells, the Dorimants and the Lady Touchwoods, in their own sphere, do not offend my moral sense; in fact they do

not appeal to it at all. They seem engaged in their
proper element. They break through no laws or conscientious restraints. They know of none. They have
got out of Christendom into the land—what shall I call
it?—of cuckoldry—the Utopia of gallantry, where pleasure is duty, and the manners perfect freedom. It is
altogether a speculative scene of things, which has no
reference whatever to the world that is. No good person can be justly offended as a spectator, because no
good person suffers on the stage. Judged morally, every
character in these plays—the few exceptions only are
mistakes—is alike essentially vain and worthless. The
great art of Congreve is especially shown in this, that
he has entirely excluded from his scenes—some little
generosities in the part of Angelica, perhaps, excepted
—not only anything like a faultless character, but any
pretensions to goodness or good feelings whatsoever.
Whether he did this designedly or instinctively, the effect
is as happy as the design (if design) was bold. I used
to wonder at the strange power which his Way of the
World in particular possesses of interesting you all along
in the pursuits of characters for whom you absolutely
care nothing—for you neither hate nor love his personages—and I think it is owing to this very indifference
for any that you endure the whole. He has spread a
privation of moral light, I will call it, rather than by
the ugly name of palpable darkness, over his creations;
and his shadows flit before you without distinction or
preference. Had he introduced a good character, a single gush of moral feeling, a revulsion of the judgment to
actual life and actual duties, the impertinent Goshen
would have only lighted to the discovery of deformities,
which now are none, because we think them none.

Translated into real life, the characters of his, and his friend Wycherley's dramas, are profligates and strumpets—the business of their brief existence the undivided pursuit of lawless gallantry. No other spring of action or possible motive of conduct is recognized; principles which, universally acted upon, must reduce this frame of things to a chaos. But we do them wrong in so translating them. No such effects are produced in *their* world. When we are among them we are among a chaotic people. We are not to judge them by our usages. No reverend institutions are insulted by their proceedings, for they have none among them. No peace of families is violated, for no family ties exist among them. No purity of the marriage-bed is stained, for none is supposed to have a being. No deep affections are disquieted, no holy wedlock bands are snapped asunder, for affection's depth and wedded faith are not of the growth of that soil. There is neither right nor wrong, gratitude or its opposite, claim or duty, paternity or sonship. Of what consequence is it to Virtue, or how is she at all concerned about it, whether Sir Simon or Dapperwit steal away Miss Martha, or who is the father of Lord Froth's or Sir Paul Pliant's children.

The whole is a passing pageant, where we should sit as unconcerned at the issues, for life or death, as at a battle of the frogs and mice. But, like Don Quixote, we take part against the puppets, and quite as impertinently. We dare not contemplate an Atlantis, a scheme, out of which our coxcombical moral sense is for a little transitory ease excluded. We have not the courage to imagine a state of things for which there is neither reward nor punishment. We cling to the painful necessities of shame and blame. We would indict our very dreams.

Amid the mortifying circumstances attendant upon growing old, it is something to have seen the School for Scandal in its glory. This comedy grew out of Congreve and Wycherley, but gathered some allays of the sentimental comedy which followed theirs. It is impossible that it should be now *acted*, though it continues, at long intervals, to be announced in the bills. Its hero, when Palmer played it, at least, was Joseph Surface. When I remember the gay boldness, the graceful, solemn plausibility, the measured step, the insinuating voice—to express it in a word—the downright *acted* villainy of the part, so different from the pressure of conscious actual wickedness—the hypocritical assumption of hypocrisy—which made Jack so deservedly a favorite in that character, I must needs conclude the present generation of playgoers more virtuous than myself, or more dense. I freely confess that he divided the palm with me with his better brother; that, in fact, I liked him quite as well. Not but there are passages—like that, for instance, where Joseph is made to refuse a pittance to a poor relation—incongruities which Sheridan was forced upon by the attempt to join the artificial with the sentimental comedy, either of which must destroy the other—but over these obstructions Jack's manner floated him so lightly that a refusal from him no more shocked you than the easy compliance of Charles gave you in reality any pleasure; you got over the paltry question as quickly as you could, to get back into the regions of pure comedy, where no cold moral reigns. The highly-artificial manner of Palmer in this character counteracted every disagreeable impression which you might have received from the contrast, supposing them real, between the two brothers. You did not believe in Joseph with the same faith with which you believed in Charles. The latter was a pleasant reality, the former a no less pleasant poetical foil to it. The comedy, I have said, is incongruous—a mixture of Congreve with sentimental incompatibilities; the gayety upon the whole is buoyant, but it required the consummate art of Palmer to reconcile the discordant elements.

A player with Jack's talents, if we had one now, would not dare to do the part in the same manner. He would instinctively avoid every turn which might tend to unrealize, and so to make the character fascinating. He must take his cue from his spectators, who would expect a bad man and a good man as rigidly opposed to each other as the death-beds of those geniuses are contrasted in the prints, which I am sorry to say have disappeared from the windows of my old friend Carrington Bowles, of St. Paul's Church-yard memory—(an exhibition as venerable as the adjacent cathedral, and almost coeval) of the bad and good man at the hour of death; where the ghastly apprehensions of the former—and truly the grim phantom, with his reality of a toasting-fork is not to be despised—so finely contrast with the meek, complacent kissing of the rod—taking it in like honey and butter—with which the latter submits to the scythe of the gentle bleeder, Time, who wields his lancet with the apprehensive finger of a popular young ladies' surgeon. What flesh, like loving grass, would not covet to meet half-way the stroke of such a delicate mower? John Palmer was twice an actor in this exquisite part. He was playing to you all the while that he was playing upon Sir Peter and his lady. You had the first intimation of a sentiment before it was on his lips. His altered voice was meant to you, and you were to suppose that

his fictitious co-flutterers on the stage perceived nothing
at all of it.   What was it to you if that half reality, the
husband, was overreached by the puppetry—or the thin
thing (Lady Teazle's reputation) was persuaded it was
dying of a plethory ?   The fortunes of Othello and Desdemona were not concerned in it.   Poor Jack has passed
from the stage in good time, that he did not live to this
our age of seriousness.   The pleasant old Teazle *King*,
too, is gone in good time.   His manner would scarce
have passed current in our day.   We must love or hate—
acquit or condemn—censure or pity—exert our detestable coxcombry of moral judgment upon everything.
Joseph Surface, to go down now, must be a downright
revolting villain—no compromise—his first appearance
must shock and give horror—his specious plausibilities,
which the pleasurable faculties of our fathers welcomed
with such hearty greetings, knowing that no harm (dramatic harm even) could come or was meant to come, of
them, must inspire a cold and killing aversion.   Charles
(the real canting person of the scene—for the hypocrisy
of Joseph has its ulterior legitimate ends, but his brother's professions of a good heart centre in downright self-
satisfaction) must be *loved*, and Joseph *hated*.   To balance
one disagreeable reality with another, Sir Peter Teazle
must be no longer the comic idea of a fretful old bachelor bridegroom, whose teasings (while King acted it)
were evidently as much played off at you, as they were
meant to concern anybody on the stage—he must be a
real person, capable in law of sustaining an injury—a
person toward whom duties are to be acknowledged—
the genuine *crim. con.* antagonist of the villainous se-
ducer Joseph.   To realize him more, his sufferings under
his unfortunate match must have the downright pun-

gency of life—must (or should) make you not mirthful but uncomfortable, just as the same predicament
would move you in a neighbor or old friend. The delicious scenes which give the play its name and zest,
must affect you in the same serious manner as if you
heard the reputation of a dear female friend attacked in
your real presence. Crabtree and Sir Benjamin—those
poor snakes that live but in the sunshine of your mirth—
must be ripened by this hot-bed process of realization
into asps or amphisbænas ; and Mrs. Candor—O ! frightful!—become a hooded serpent. Oh ! who that remem-
bers Parsons and Dodd—the wasp and butterfly of the
School for Scandal—in those two characters ; and charming natural Miss Pope, the perfect gentlewoman, as dis-
tinguished from the fine lady of comedy, in this latter
part—would forego the true scenic delight—the escape
from life—the oblivion of consequences—the holiday
barring out of the pedant Reflection—those Saturnalia
of two or three brief hours, well won from the world—
to sit instead at one of our modern plays—to have his
coward conscience (that, forsooth, must not be left for
a moment) stimulated with perpetual appeals — dulled
rather, and blunted, as a faculty without repose must
be—and his moral vanity pampered with images of notional justice, notional beneficence, lives saved without
the spectator's risk, and fortunes given away that cost
the author nothing ?

No piece was, perhaps, ever so completely cast in all
its parts as this *manager's comedy*. Miss Farren had
succeeded to Mrs. Abington in Lady Teazle; and Smith,
the original Charles, had retired when I first saw it.
The rest of the characters, with very slight exceptions,
remained. I remember it was then the fashion to cry

down John Kemble, who took the part of Charles after Smith; but, I thought, very unjustly. Smith, I fancy, was more airy, and took the eye with a certain gayety of person. He brought with him no sombre recollections of tragedy. He had not to expiate the fault of having pleased beforehand in lofty declamation. He had no sins of Hamlet or of Richard to atone for. His failure in these parts was a passport to success in one of so opposite a tendency. But, as far as I could judge, the weighty sense of Kemble made up for more personal incapacity than he had to answer for. His harshest tones in this part came steeped and dulcified in good-humor. He made his defects a grace. His exact declamatory manner, as he managed it, only served to convey the points of his dialogue with more precision. It seemed to head the shafts to carry them deeper. Not one of his sparkling sentences was lost. I remember minutely how he delivered each in succession, and cannot by any effort imagine how any of them could be altered for the better. No man could deliver brilliant dialogue—the dialogue of Congreve or of Wycherley—because none understood it—half so well as John Kemble. His Valentine, in Love for Love, was, to my recollection, faultless. He flagged sometimes in the intervals of tragic passion. He would slumber over the level parts of an heroic character. His Macbeth has been known to nod. But he always seemed to me to be particularly alive to pointed and witty dialogue. The relaxing levities of tragedy have not been touched by any since him—the playful, court-bred spirit in which he condescended to the players in Hamlet—the sportive relief which he threw into the darker shades of Richard—disappeared with him. He had his sluggish moods, his torpors—but they were the halting-stones and resting-place of his tragedy—politic savings, and fetches of the breath—husbandry of the lungs, where Nature pointed him to be an economist—rather, I think, than errors of the judgment. They were, at worst, less painful than the eternal, tormenting, unappeasable vigilance—the "lidless dragon-eyes" of present fashionable tragedy.

ON THE ACTING OF MUNDEN.

NOT many nights ago, I had come home from seeing this extraordinary performer in Cockletop; and when I retired to my pillow, his whimsical image still stuck by me, in a manner as to threaten sleep. In vain I tried to divest myself of it, by conjuring up the most opposite associations. I resolved to be serious. I raised up the gravest topics of life; private misery, public calamity. All would not do:

—"There the antic sate
Mocking our state "—

his queer visnomy—his bewildering costume—all the strange things which he had raked together—his serpentine rod, swagging about in his pocket—Cleopatra's tear, and the rest of his relics—O'Keefe's wild farce, and his wilder commentary—till the passion of laughter, like grief in excess, relieved itself by its own weight, inviting the sleep which, in the first instance, it had driven away.

But I was not to escape so easily. No sooner did I fall into slumbers, than the same image, only more per-

plexing, assailed me in the shape of dreams. Not one
Munden, but five hundred, were dancing before me, like
the faces which, whether you will or no, come when you
have been taking opium—all the strange combinations,
which this strangest of all strange mortals ever shot his
proper countenance into, from the day he came commissioned to dry up the tears of the town for the loss of the
now almost forgotten Edwin.   O for the power of the
pencil to have fixed them when I awoke!   A season or
two since, there was exhibited a Hogarth gallery.   I do
not see why there should not be a Munden gallery.   In
richness and variety, the latter would not fall far short
of the former.

There is one face of Farley, one face of Knight, one
(but what a one it is!) of Liston; but Munden has none
that you can properly pin down, and call *his*.   When you
think he has exhausted his battery of looks, in unac-
countable warfare with your gravity, suddenly he sprouts
out an entirely new set of features, like Hydra.   He is
not one, but legion; not so much a comedian as a company.   If his name could be multiplied like his countenance, it might fill a play-bill.   He, and he alone, literally *makes faces;* applied to any other person, the phrase
is a mere figure, denoting certain modifications of the
human countenance.   Out of some invisible wardrobe
he dips for faces, as his friend Suett used for wigs, and
fetches them out as easily.   I should not be surprised to
see him some day put out the head of a river-horse; or
come forth a pewitt, or lapwing, some feathered meta-
morphosis.

I have seen this gifted actor in Sir Christopher Curry
—in old Dornton—diffuse a glow of sentiment which has
made the pulse of a crowded theatre beat like that of one

man; when he has come in aid of the pulpit, doing good to the moral heart of a people, I have seen some faint approaches to this sort of excellence in other players. But in the grand grotesque of farce, Munden stands out as single and unaccompanied as Hogarth. Hogarth, strange to tell, had no followers. The school of Munden began, and must end, with himself.

Can any man *wonder* like him? can any man *see ghosts* like him? or *fight with his own shadow*—" SESSA " —as he does in that strangely-neglected thing, the Cobbler of Preston—where his alternations from the Cobbler to the Magnifico, and from the Magnifico to the Cobbler, keep the brain of the spectator in as wild a ferment as if some Arabian Night were being acted before him. Who, like him, can throw, or ever attempted to throw, a preternatural interest over the commonest daily-life objects? A table, or a joint-stool, in his conception, rises into a dignity equivalent to Cassiopeia's chair. It is invested with constellatory importance. You could not speak of it with more deference, if it were mounted into the firmament. A beggar in the hands of Michael Angelo, says Fuseli, rose the Patriarch of Poverty. So the gusto of Munden antiquates and ennobles what it touches. His pots and his ladles are as grand and primal as the seething-pots and hooks seen in old prophetic vision. A tub of butter, contemplated by him, amounts to a Platonic idea. He understands a leg of mutton in its quiddity. He stands wondering, amid the commonplace materials of life, like primeval man with the sun and stars about him.

THE END.

Milton Keynes UK
Ingram Content Group UK Ltd.
UKHW051920140823
426877UK00005B/198